Kazuo Ishiguro's
The Remains of the Day

CONTINUUM CONTEMPORARIES

Also available in this series

Forthcoming in this series

· **KAZUO ISHIGURO'S**

The Remains of the Day

A READER'S GUIDE

ADAM PARKES

CONTINUUM | NEW YORK | LONDON

2001

The Continuum International Publishing Group Inc
370 Lexington Avenue, New York, NY 10017

The Continuum International Publishing Group Ltd
The Tower Building, 11 York Road, London SE1 7NX

Printed in the United States of America

Library of Congress Cataloging-in-Publication Data

Parkes, Adam, 1966–
    Kazuo Ishiguro's The remains of the day / Adam Parkes.
       p.   cm. — (Continuum contemporaries)
    Includes bibliographical references and index.
    ISBN 0-8264-5231-0 (alk. paper)
    1. Ishiguro, Kazuo, 1954– . Remains of the day.   2. Master and
servant in literature.   3. Country homes in literature.   4. Domestics in
literature.   I. Title.   II. Series.
   PR6059.S5 R4637 2001
   823'.914—dc21

                                                2001028694

for my parents, David and Maggie

and

my sisters, Clare and Lisa

Contents

Acknowledgments

While writing this book I have enjoyed the benefit of helpful conversations with several people, especially two of my colleagues at the University of Georgia, Simon Gatrell and Hubert Mc-Alexander, and my parents-in-law, Peter and Nancy Mattern. Many thanks, too, to my editor at Continuum, David Barker, who has seen this book through from its inception to its completion. My greatest debt of all is to my wife (and colleague), Susan Mattern-Parkes; I am grateful to her for everything.

1

The Novelist

Kazuo Ishiguro was born in Nagasaki, Japan, on November 8, 1954. In 1960 the five-year-old Ishiguro moved with his family to Britain, where his father, an oceanographer, began a one-year research project funded by the British government. What was originally intended to be a temporary visit gradually became a permanent one; while maintaining ownership of the family home in Nagasaki, the Ishiguros have remained in Britain. Ishiguro and his two sisters enjoyed what he has described as a typical middle-class English upbringing in Guildford, Surrey. After attending a local grammar school, Ishiguro studied English and Philosophy at the University of Kent at Canterbury, graduating with a B.A. with Honors in 1978. The next year he traveled in North America; on returning to Britain, he undertook sundry occupations, and even flirted with the idea of becoming a singer-songwriter. He also worked for the Cyrenians, an independent welfare organization that helps the homeless and unemployed. It was through his social work, which he resumed briefly in the early 1980s, that Ishiguro met his wife, Lorna Anne MacDougall. Ishiguro and Lorna married in

1986, and they now live in London with their daughter, Naomi, who was born in 1992.

Ishiguro took his first steps toward a literary career in 1979 when he entered the Creative Writing program at the University of East Anglia. His teachers at East Anglia included the novelist and critic Malcolm Bradbury and the fabulist Angela Carter. After receiving his M.A. in 1980, Ishiguro wrote short stories and television scripts: *A Profile of Arthur J. Mason* was screened by Channel Four in 1984, followed by *The Gourmet* in 1986. In 1981, three of Ishiguro's stories—"A Strange and Sometimes Sadness," "Waiting for J," and "Getting Poisoned"—appeared in *Introduction 7: Stories by New Writers*, a Faber and Faber series designed to bring young authors before a wider reading public. In Ishiguro's case, exposure to a large readership was not far off. In 1982, the year he became a British citizen, Faber published *A Pale View of Hills*, the first of five award-winning novels that have brought him worldwide fame. This delicately handled but unsettling tale of a middle-aged Japanese woman, who survived the Nagasaki atomic bomb and now lives in an English village, won the Royal Society of Literature's Winifred Holtby Prize, and thus established Ishiguro on the British literary map. This was followed by the Whitbread Book of the Year Award for *An Artist of the Floating World* (1986), another novel set in Japan but narrated this time by an aging former artist, Masuji Ono, who struggles to come to terms with the new conditions of postwar life.

Each of Ishiguro's early novels was translated into several languages, but his fame in the English-speaking world was limited, for the most part, to Britain. This situation changed in 1989 with the publication of his third novel, *The Remains of the Day*, which won Britain's most prestigious literary award, the Booker Prize, and the appearance of the Knopf edition (the text cited in the present work), which brought accolades from American reviewers as well. Like

Ishiguro's first two novels, *Remains* is the first-person retrospective account of an aging narrator, and again the lucid, tightly-controlled narrative is remarkable for its deftness and a beguiling simplicity of surface that expresses subtly interwoven themes of pain and loss. The subject of this novel, however, is only indirectly related to the issues of Japanese history that are elaborated in *Pale View* and *Artist*. *Remains* is set in England, and England is its preeminent subject, as seen through the eyes of Stevens, the butler at Darlington Hall (a fictional stately home located near Oxford), who looks back over a life that he devoted to serving a now infamous Nazi sympathizer of the 1930s. In addition to introducing such emphatically English subject-matter, *Remains* is also the first Ishiguro novel that may be considered a love story—although it would be more precise, per-haps, to call it the story of a love story that never quite happens. Fueled by the interest generated by the immensely popular Merchant-Ivory film adaptation of 1993, *Remains* became an inter-national bestseller, with more than a million copies sold in the English language alone.

Remains has been followed by two more novels—*The Uncon-soled* (1995), a surrealistic masterpiece, and most recently *When We Were Orphans* (2000), in which Ishiguro returns (with questionable success) to the style of the first three works. In *The Unconsoled* the narrator is a world-famous concert pianist called Ryder, who finds himself in an unnamed Central European city where he is expected to take part in an important but unspecified public performance, while numerous characters (including his own family) make end-less, indeed impossible, demands on his time, which leave him and the reader feeling that life's consolations are always out of reach. *When We Were Orphans*, which was short-listed for the Booker Prize, is the tale of a famous English detective, Christopher Banks, who moves back and forth (in time and in space) between England and the Shanghai of his youth in the years between the two world wars. Meanwhile, Ishiguro has continued to be showered with prizes. In 1995 alone he received Italy's Premio Scanno, the Cheltenham Prize, and an O.B.E. (Order of the British Empire) for Services to Literature. He has been awarded honorary doctorates by the Universities of Kent (1990) and East Anglia (1995), and in 1998 he received the French decoration Chevalier de l'Ordre des Arts et des Lettres.

Ishiguro has often been characterized as one of the leading lights of a new generation of British (or British-resident) writers—a generation that includes Martin Amis, Julian Barnes, Ian McEwan, Timothy Mo, Ben Okri, Salman Rushdie, Graham Swift, and Jeannette Winterson. As Ishiguro himself has pointed out, he is frequently linked with two particular members of this group—the Chinese-British novelist Mo and Indian-born Rushdie—because each of them has a non-British ancestry that he explores in his fiction. Ishiguro has suggested that Rushdie, in winning the Booker Prize for his novel about the birth of India, *Midnight's Children* (1981), paved the way for Ishiguro's own success, because he drew attention to new multicultural possibilities for fiction at a time when the novel in Britain seemed to be in serious decline. What unites this generation of writers, Ishiguro claimed in an interview in 1991, "is the consciousness that Britain is not the center of the universe." Since the break-up of its empire at the end of the Second World War, Ishiguro remarks, Britain has had to face its increasing cultural marginality in relation to the rest of the world, and its writers have only just begun to find ways of adjusting their fictional lenses to this new historical situation. For Ishiguro himself, this means attempting to reach a more "international" audience by abandoning subject-matter that appeals only to a "provincial" British reader.

But apart from conceding this broadly shared preoccupation with expanding British cultural horizons, Ishiguro resists further attempts to group him with the likes of Rushdie and Mo, and he is right to do so. Ishiguro's style, as he observes in the same interview, is quite different from theirs. Rushdie's language is explosive and exploratory, "chas[ing] after something just beyond the reach of words"; Ishiguro's own language is deliberately restrained and elegantly understated, "the sort that actually suppresses meaning and tries to hide away meaning." While Rushdie's narrative structures, multiplying the levels of reality inhabited by his characters, feel improvisational and sometimes outrageously experimental, the "spare, tight" structure of an Ishiguro novel seems disarmingly straightforward and conventional by comparison. Ishiguro says that in his own work he tries to avoid, or at least disguise, the postmodern elements that readers have come to expect of Rushdie's novels.

One way of gauging more accurately Ishiguro's place in modern literature is to compare him with Chekhov and Dostoevsky, the great Russian writers whom he described, in a 1989 interview with fellow-novelist Graham Swift, as the "two god-like figures in my reading experience." Ishiguro has often claimed Chekhov as a key influence on his work, and so far, he explains, it is Chekhov that he has tried to emulate, especially his spare precision and "the carefully controlled tone." Ishiguro points to the slow pace and relative unimportance of plot in his own novels as marks of Chekhov's influence: "I try to put in as little plot as possible," he told another interviewer in 1990. The steady, unhurried focus on ordinary life is another notable point of contact with this Russian precursor. And yet, Ishiguro confesses, "I do sometimes envy the utter mess, the chaos of Dostoevsky." Here Ishiguro is probably referring not to Dostoevsky's plots, which (somewhat like Chekhov's) tend toward simplicity, but to the world of psychological and spiritual extremity that we encounter in Dostoevsky's often overwrought characters. Ishiguro adds that he feels the pressure of this "messy, chaotic, undisciplined" element from within his own "writing self" — an element that he regards as virtually absent from his previous fiction, but that he now wishes to explore.

Signs of this Dostoevskian element are present in several of Ishiguro's works. One of his stories, "Getting Poisoned" (a pastiche, he has said, of early Ian McEwan), is the fictional diary of a psychopathic adolescent who poisons first his cat and then, just at the moment when he is about to have sex with her, the teenaged daughter of his mother's live-in boyfriend. In another story, "Waiting for J," a deranged university teacher describes his terror as he awaits the mysterious J, whom he murdered four years ago in grisly fulfilment of an agreement supposedly made in jest; ignoring the laws of physical possibility, the narrator fears that his victim might return to keep up his end of the bargain. Eschewing the sex and violence of these early efforts, Ishiguro discovered another way to express his "messy, chaotic, undisciplined" side in the surrealism of *The Unconsoled*, a novel that provokes irremediable anxiety in one form after another, and in ways that invariably elude the narrator's control. There is an extravagance and restlessness about *The Unconsoled* that seems to respond to the new imperative to leave aside the discipline and order of the early novels.

Yet the style of *The Unconsoled* is also distinguished by many of the traits and tendencies that characterize the first three novels and, most recently, *When We Were Orphans*. Once again, Ishiguro writes in a plain economical style whose limpid grace works by nuance and implication; again, a first-person narrator is employed to "develop the whole business about following somebody's thoughts around" (as he put it in one interview). If there is a new influence at work in *The Unconsoled*, it is Kafka, especially the angst-ridden Kafka of *The Trial* (1925), rather than Dostoevsky, to whom Ishiguro is no closer in spirit than he is to Rushdie. Rushdie is indeed a much closer postmodern equivalent to Dostoevsky, a point suggested by the verbal similarities that may be observed in Ishiguro's portraits of these two writers (the "mess" and "chaos" associated with Dostoevsky reappears in Ishiguro's account of the "terrific energy" of Rushdie's novels). In Ishiguro, the affinity with Chekhov goes much deeper.

Ishiguro's stylistic affinity with Chekhov is confirmed by his admiration for American writers such as Ernest Hemingway, Raymond Carver, and Richard Ford, who explore the expressive potential of silence in a manner reminiscent of (if not directly influenced by) their Russian precursor. With Carver and Ford, moreover, Ishiguro shares Chekhov's assiduous concern with everyday life, or what Ford, in his introduction to *The Essential Tales of Chekhov* (1998), calls the "mapping out degree by precise degree an accurate, ground-level constellation of ordinary existence." By contrast, metafictional authors such as Thomas Pynchon, William Gass, and John Barth hold little interest for Ishiguro, who doesn't believe "that the nature of fiction is one of the burning issues of the late twentieth century": "reading Ford and Carver for me is a kind of antidote really to those over-intellectualized or self-conscious literary creations that almost seem to be created for the professor down the corridor to decipher." Ishiguro's preference for fiction that represents the quotidian world of ordinary people—the world of butlers, for example, is meant to be everyone's world—has diverted him from the metafictional route that authors find themselves traveling (he says) once they include writers among their characters. "I think it's always dangerous to have a writer in a novel," Ishiguro remarks. "I try to avoid that very postmodern element in my books."

Where, then, does Ishiguro stand in relation to the tradition that exercised the greatest formative influence over his literary education—the tradition of British literature? In an effort, perhaps, to emphasize the messy, chaotic aspect of his "writing self," Ishiguro has claimed Charlotte Brontë and Charles Dickens as two of his major British influences, but it would be difficult to pick a pair of writers with weaker correspondences to his own narrative style. The British novelists with whom Ishiguro has the strongest affinities are Henry James, an expatriate American who eventually became a British citizen, and Ford Madox Ford. Like both of these precursors, Ishiguro is preoccupied, even obsessed, with the nature of consciousness. Stylistically, Ishiguro has relatively little in common with James, but every one of Ishiguro's novels takes up the quintessential Jamesian task of tracing the sinuous operations of the human mind — of "following somebody's thoughts around" to reveal the depths of self-deception we are prepared to plumb as we evade the truth about ourselves. Ishiguro shares other concerns with James, most notably the theme of exile, which for each writer is rooted in the personal experience of geographical and cultural displacement, but at the deepest level it is consciousness that fascinates them both. Ishiguro's plots — or what we should properly call his anti-plots — conform quite closely to the structural and thematic map of several of James's novels and stories, such as "The Beast in the Jungle" (first published in 1903), whose narrator, John Marcher, finds that in waiting for the great event that will change his life he misses out on life itself. Like so many of James's protagonists, and like many other characters in modern literature who bear the mark of James's influence (T. S. Eliot's J. Alfred Prufrock is a prominent example), Ishiguro's characters are gripped so intensely by the life of the mind that they are paralyzed by it; they can think, but they can't act.

Ishiguro's affinity with Ford is, if anything, even stronger than that with James. Ford's impressionist masterpiece, *The Good Soldier* (1915), employs the diction and syntax of an apparently normal educated middle-class man (the narrator, John Dowell) in an exploration of consciousness that is intimately connected to problems of narrative and memory. This is precisely the terrain that Ishiguro has set out to explore—a terrain that he describes as "terribly treacherous" because full of "ambiguities" that "feed self-deception." In the background of Ford's novel, though it is never stated, is the Great War, which broke out while Ford was writing; similarly, Ishiguro's novels make us feel the psychological and emotional consequences of the Second World War, but often without directly referring to it. Like Ishiguro after him, moreover, Ford is deeply concerned with the discordant relationship between the world that exists inside the confused mind of his traumatized narrator, on one hand, and, on the other hand, an external reality that seems perpetually to elude Dowell's grasp: Dowell's account of the events leading up to the collapse of his marriage and the death of his best friend, the "good soldier" Edward Ashburnham, never coheres as a consistent or reliable picture of external reality, although it tells us a lot about his psyche. Memory, in other words, has got the better of Dowell, and the same is true of Ishiguro's protagonists. Like *The Good Soldier*, Ishiguro's novels communicate what he calls the "texture of memory," which means that sometimes the mess and chaos of ordinary life never gets cleaned up. On the contrary, what we see is the imaginative work that we silently perform—registered in the ellipses, obscurities, repetitions of our own speech—as we talk ourselves into believing the stories that we want to believe. Ironically, it is by cultivating what he calls his Chekhovian side—the elegant and deceptively simple language that aligns him with Ford Madox Ford—that Ishiguro most completely fulfills his openly acknowledged desire to write about the side of life found in Dostoevsky. For it is this language that allows him to express the turbulent darkness that exists on the other side of the beautifully polished yet flawed mirrors of his narrators' stories.

To compare Ishiguro with James and Ford is to acknowledge Ishiguro's debt to the modernist tradition in English letters, which replaced the devotion to factual detail that prevailed in much nineteenth-century realist fiction with a new psychological realism. According to the traditional realist dispensation, the artist's duty is to hold up a mirror to nature. A novelist writing in the realist tradition is committed to representing reality, in all its manifold detail, with a quasi-scientific interest in what are regarded as objective facts — a plight that George Eliot famously described in *Adam Bede* (1859) as an obligation to "creep servilely after nature and fact [. . .] dreading nothing, indeed, but falsity." Ishiguro says that he does little historical research for his novels because he is not concerned with such "journalistic accuracy" (as he called it in an interview in 1998); he has stressed repeatedly that it is a mistake to read his novels as guides to life in postwar Japan or the social history of Britain between the world wars. Instead, like James, Ford, and other modern novelists, Ishiguro is interested primarily in the workings of language and consciousness.

At some point it becomes misleading, of course, to posit such a neat division between a devotion to material fact and an interest in consciousness: the attempt to portray reality as it appears to the human mind, or to capture the operations of the mind itself, still constitutes a kind of realism (hence the term "pyschological realism"). This, to be sure, was George Eliot's point: "I aspire to give no more than a faithful account of men and things as they have mirrored themselves in my mind. The mirror is doubtless defective; the outlines will sometimes be disturbed; the reflection faint or confused; but I feel as much bound to tell you, as precisely as I can, what that reflection is, as if I were in the witness-box narrating my experience on oath." If the realist novelist vows to tell the truth, the whole truth, and nothing but the truth, that promise is dependent on the quality of the mirror that she holds up to nature, and as that mirror is her own mind, we should be under no illusions as to its potential for omniscience or objectivity. Ishiguro expresses the same objection when bemoaning a "certain kind of misreader," who takes his second novel, *An Artist of the Floating World*, "to be simply some kind of realist text telling you what Tokyo was like after the war." But we should remember Eliot's words before leaping to the simplistic conclusion that Ishiguro's work transcends realism, except insofar as he joins modernist authors like James and Ford in developing a narrative style adequate to the task of representing reality as it is apprehended by the human mind. For all the literary propaganda in the modernist era and in our own, there is nothing innately anti-realist about modernist psychological narrative. Modern psychological realism does no more than extend the basic principles of realism to reflect the "mirror" of the human mind, and it was George Eliot who indicated the direction such an extension might take.

Ishiguro's expressions of frustration at "realist" misreading, however, are not simply a function of his own misunderstanding of literary realism; they indicate also his resistance to readers who have displayed a sometimes embarrassing enthusiasm for the "Japanese" angle that his work seems to open up for the British novel. Ishiguro frankly admits that the combination of superficiality, naivety, and condescension that make up such attitudes may have helped him to gain an early foothold in the British literary world. Some of the critical commentary in this vein is, indeed, almost comical: in the March 1986 issue of *Books and Bookmen*, for instance, a picture of a youthful Ishiguro is accompanied by the words, "distinctively Japanese delicacy." Ishiguro's insistence that he writes in the Western tradition, along with his invocation of such unlikely names as Brontë and Dickens, is probably intended to deter readers from seeing his novels as guidebooks to modern Japan, or as the mouthpieces of a "Japanese" point of view.

A strong case may be made, nonetheless, for linking Ishiguro's work to various aspects of Japanese culture, especially modern writers such as Masuji Ibuse, Yasunari Kawabata, Natsume Soseki, and Junichiro Tanizaki. In interviews Ishiguro has sometimes downplayed his affinities with these authors, but in his fiction their influence is often palpable. One likely source of such influence is Soseki's *Kokoro* (1914; English translation, 1957), a first-person retrospective narrative about a master-pupil relationship that foreshadows the life of Masuji Ono in *An Artist of the Floating World*, as well as Stevens's relationship to Lord Darlington in *The Remains of the Day*. Like some of his own British contemporaries, such as Conrad and Ford Madox Ford, as well as Ishiguro after him, Soseki dwells on themes of loneliness, time's passing, and the conflict between modern and traditional ways of life. In Ishiguro's favorite Tanizaki novel, *Diary of a Mad Old Man* (1961–62; English translation, 1965), we find one of the models for his own diary narratives. In his overt preoccupation with sexual fantasy, Tanizaki's diaristnarrator, Utsugi, represents everything that is elided by Stevens in *Remains*, but for this very reason Utsugi might be regarded as Stevens's repressed double. Similar speculations are provoked by *The Key* (1956; English translation, 1961), in which Tanizaki exploits the erotic implications of multiple diaries. The possibilities of the diary form are also explored in Ibuse's powerful novel about the bombing of Hiroshima, *Black Rain* (1966; English translation, 1969), whose vivid dramatic content is subtly remembered in the silences and ellipses of Ishiguro's narrator, Etsuko, as she picks over the remains of postwar Nagasaki in *A Pale View of Hills*.

Ishiguro's Introduction to a 1986 British edition of Kawabata's short novels *Snow Country* and *Thousand Cranes* forces us to consider his relationship to modern Japanese literature in a slightly different way. Ishiguro cautions the Western reader against assuming that Kawabata's characters seem strange merely because they appear in Japanese novels: "Of course, you *will* find characters behaving oddly and obsessively," Ishiguro remarks, "but this is more likely to be because they are characters in a Kawabata novel, rather than because they are Japanese." Ishiguro also insists, however, on Kawabata's place in a " 'classical' tradition of Japanese prose-writing pre-dating the influence of European realism—a tradition which placed value on lyricism, mood and reflection rather than on plot and character." According to Ishiguro, Kawabata treats plot "in the Western sense" as a low priority: "Kawabata needs to be read *slowly*, the atmospheres savoured, the characters' words pondered for their nuances." Kawabata both is and is not distinctively Japanese, and when he is most Japanese he sounds like Chekhov, as well as Ishiguro himself. The point that needs to be made here is that Ishiguro is drawn to various Western and Japanese writers who emphasize character and atmosphere over plot or action. Whether or not Ishiguro's work shows signs of actual Japanese influence (ultimately, the case is impossible to prove either way), it seems to be a place where traditions that are usually supposed to be alien to each other are brought into close proximity.

Ishiguro's work betrays its connections with Japanese culture in other ways, too. It is especially profitable, as Gregory Mason has shown, to read Ishiguro's early novels in the light of Japanese film, particularly a modern genre called *shomin-geki*, which somewhat resembles the Western soap opera. "It's concerned with ordinary people in everyday life," Ishiguro explains, "and it has that sort of pace: a pace which reflects the monotony and melancholy of every-day life. It's almost like some Western travel-writing in its disparateness, its impressionistic way of describing a character just going through life, having ideas about different things." The main difference between the *shomin-geki* and the soap opera is the rela-tive absence of plot that characterizes the Japanese form—hence its appeal to Ishiguro, who says, half-jokingly, that he's trying to phase plot out. The point of the *shomin-geki*, for Ishiguro, is that it situates characters firmly in the context of the quotidian world, instead of subordinating them to the demand for plot that predominates in the Western tradition. In the West, Ishiguro told one interviewer, we tend to assume that "plot has to do with taking people out of the ordinary and mundane, and the story usually resolves with the hero returning to ordinary life. The plot is all about the detour." What Ishiguro means to do in his own fiction is to trace the main journey in order to "see below the surface of everyday life to the emotions and what makes people do what they do." The nearest Western equivalent, he observes, is Chekhov.

The Japanese strain in Ishiguro's work, then, is not a matter of conveying direct knowledge of Japan itself, but one of reworking previous representations of Japan, including representations by Japanese as well as Western artists. Another reason for Ishiguro's attraction to the *shomin-geki* is that it frustrates common Western expectations about Japanese life — expectations courted by Mishima, whose work, life, and death have perpetuated the European stereotype of the suicidal Japanese. At some level, Ishiguro's novels may be read as a concerted effort to subvert such stereotypical assumptions because they decline to provide the dramatic climax that suicide guarantees. Ishiguro performs this revisionary work by making his readers feel the pressure of the suicidal cliché, and then quietly refusing to deliver it. The short story "A Family Supper," first published in 1983, illustrates this point. Over dinner one night a Japanese family discusses the father's former business colleague, who has died (probably intentionally) by his own hand. Will the father, too, commit suicide? Nothing of the sort happens; the family simply finishes its meal. The effect of this dénouement is precisely the opposite of that produced by the tales of Ishiguro's former teacher, Angela Carter. In Carter's fiction, as Michael Wood writes in his book *Children of Silence* (1998), we encounter a "fictional psychopathology of everyday life" that points "to the persistent, lurid reality of so many fantasies." In contrast, Ishiguro's fiction reveals the fantastic, or mythical, elements lurking in our notions of every-day reality—including the complacent idea that while we are entirely ordinary, other people routinely perform grotesque variations on the theme of self-destruction.

Each of Ishiguro's first two novels raises these issues. At the beginning of A *Pale View of Hills* the narrator, Etsuko, is thinking about her Japanese daughter, Keiko, who has recently committed suicide. Casting her mind back to a long hot summer after the Second World War, Etsuko recalls traumatic stories of child-murder and suicide, which are interlaced with her daughter's death by a series of subtle yet haunting rope-images (Keiko hanged herself). We may wonder at the end whether Etsuko, too, is about to kill herself: the novel concludes with Etsuko standing at the door, smiling and waving goodbye to her English daughter, Niki. A similar suspicion attaches to Masuji Ono, the aging Japanese former artist who narrates Ishiguro's second novel, An *Artist of the Floating World*. Here, again, suicide abounds, as Japan's former leaders atone in violent fashion for bringing their nation to its knees. Will Ono do likewise? Ishiguro teases us with this possibility, but only to reveal the ways in which our anticipation of such an outcome has as much to do with Western stereotypes about Japan as with actual evidence. As Etsuko remarks of newspaper accounts of Keiko's death in *Pale View*: "The English are fond of their idea that our race has an instinct for suicide, as if further explanations are unnecessary; for that was all they reported, that she was Japanese and that she had hung herself in her room."

Ishiguro's larger point is that "people are just seen to be people": "I ask myself the same questions about my Japanese characters that I would about English characters," he says. "My experience of Japanese people in this realm is that they're like everybody else. They're like me, my parents. I don't see them as people who go around slashing their stomachs." Ishiguro's sole return visit to Japan in 1989 confirmed his apprehension that he knew very little about the historical modern Japan. What he tries to convey in his representations of Japan is a discernable similarity to the real Japan that is not quite an identity; the reader should feel a sense of difference, or slippage, which reveals Ishiguro's "Japan" as a country invented, "out of little scraps, out of memories, out of speculation, out of imagination," for ends other than fidelity to literal fact. Ishiguro's Japan is like Stevens's England in *The Remains of the Day*, or Ryder's Central European city in *The Unconsoled*, or Banks's Shanghai in *When We Were Orphans*: a stage that drifts free of its moorings in historical reality, a floating world, on which the characters enact dramas about universal themes.

Ishiguro's major themes are the ordinary experience of loss and time's passing; the shifts in moral and political perspective that time's passing brings and that renders what once seemed dignified or honorable merely anachronistic, or even (as in *Artist* and *Remains*) criminal; treachery, betrayal, and the difficulties of reconciliation; conflict between generations; and, most importantly, the nature of history and myth. Ishiguro's exploration of the problem of history causes him to traverse the rocky terrain of various, though related, sub-themes: exile, homelessness, nostalgia, and nationalism. Commenting on the sense of artistic opportunity that results from his "very lack of authority and lack of knowledge about Japan," Ishiguro told the Japanese novelist and Nobel Laureate Kenzaburo Oe that he thinks of himself "as a kind of homeless writer": "I had no obvious social role, because I wasn't a very English Englishman, and I wasn't a very Japanese Japanese either.[. . .] Nobody's history seemed to be my history." In *The Remains of the Day*, as in his other novels, Ishiguro translates this sense of homelessness into a compelling representation of the everyday world that tells a similar, but tellingly different, story about the human condition. In the floating worlds of Ishiguro's fiction, "nobody's history" is everyone's history.

2

The Novel

STORIES

The *Remains of the Day* is, on the face of it, a simple story. Like its immediate predecessor, *An Artist of the Floating World*, it is written in the form of a diary, but whereas the previous novel's narration spans two years in the period after the end of the Second World War (from October 1948 to June 1950), *Remains* covers a much shorter period: six days in July 1956. The story is told by Stevens, the elderly butler of Darlington Hall near Oxford, who undertakes a six-day excursion to the English West Country that takes him first to Salisbury, then Dorset, Somerset, Devon, and Cornwall, before ending in Weymouth. Stevens is traveling at the urging of Darlington Hall's new American owner, Mr. Farraday, who has even lent him his Ford automobile. The purpose of Stevens's trip is to visit his old friend Miss Kenton, the former housekeeper at Darlington Hall, who left twenty years ago to marry another man. Ostensibly, Stevens's intentions are entirely professional; Miss Kenton's expertise, he says, is badly needed at Darlington Hall, whose staff has dwindled to a mere four, compared with the twenty-eight servants employed there during its heyday. It is clear, though, that Stevens's real, if unacknowledged, motive is romantic. He wants to see Miss Kenton again in the hope of reigniting the affection she showed him twenty years ago—an affection that he foolishly and cruelly declined to return at the time. Stevens's journey to the West Country, which occurs in present chronological time and in actual geographical space, is mirrored by (and is a metaphor for) a journey of remembrance that takes him back to the Twenties and Thirties.

Weaving back and forth between the past and the present, Stevens tells another story as well: the story of his former employer, Lord Darlington. Stevens reveres Lord Darlington, and portrays him as an ideal gentleman. Again, however, Stevens reveals himself to be the unwitting victim of self-inflicted blindness, for it emerges that Lord Darlington is anything but the paragon of virtue for which Stevens has taken him; on the contrary, he is widely regarded as a Nazi sympathizer and a traitor. During the 1920s Stevens's employer, shocked by the vindictiveness with which the victorious Allies treated their defeated enemy in the Treaty of Versailles (1919–1920), played a leading role in bringing together important statesmen from the various Western powers to foster an atmosphere of mutual understanding and sympathy. Lord Darlington's intention, which Stevens regards as noble and honorable, was to prevent a recurrence of the First World War. But in the 1930s the Nazis exploited his good will and turned him into a pawn of their foreign policy; by the time the Second World War ended, Lord Darlington was in disgrace, and he died a broken man. Stevens is so full of admiration for the noble role adopted by his employer that even now he finds it difficult to fathom the contempt in which Lord Darlington is held. This difficulty is compounded by the fact that Stevens has derived considerable pride from serving a man who played such a visible role in directing the course of history—the next best thing, Stevens seems to feel, to directing it oneself. His journey in time, therefore, also represents his attempt to come to terms with the fact that his long years of professional service, from which he has drawn enormous vicarious satisfaction, have been devoted to a man whose political naivety and moral weakness helped to bring his country — indeed the whole world — to the brink of destruction.

The title of the novel brings these central themes into clear focus. On one level "the remains of the day" refers to what is left of Stevens's life: one's final years, he reflects, are supposed to be the best of all, because it is then that one is able to put one's feet up and look back with satisfaction at a life well spent. This points to another of the title's implications: what is meant by "day" is the glorious past, when Lord Darlington's fame was at its height, and Stevens himself was at the peak of his profession. (In this sense, "day" denotes a whole era.) There is a simple irony in Stevens's metaphor, however, which forces us to consider less glorious interpretations. The more Stevens tells us that his days have been well spent, the more we doubt it. While we might take the "remains" of Stevens's day to signify what persists or endures of his past life, we might view them also as its ruins or corpse. Stevens's entire narration might be characterized as a stumbling endeavor to salvage something valuable, or at least defensible, from a life that he suspects has been wasted.

Stevens's attempt to piece together his past, and to integrate it with his present, is the real substance of the novel. The literal journey from Darlington Hall to the West Country is a narrative device for dramatizing the more important journey that he makes at the level of consciousness. Ishiguro reinforces this point by locating all the significant action in the past, unfolding it only via the memories and speculations of the reflecting narrator. In this way, Ishiguro continues the surreptitious assault on dramatic content that began with *A Pale View of Hills* and extends as far as *The Unconsoled* (*When We Were Orphans*, by contrast, contains a strong present-tense story line and several scenes of vivid action). This assault is part of the commitment to "slow and almost plotless" narratives that Ishiguro sees as his link to Chekhov, and it is in the context of this commitment that the thwarted love story of *The Remains of the Day* should be understood. Stevens's suppression of his love for Miss Kenton is a ploy to divert the reader's attention to the action that takes place in the narrator's consciousness—the journey Stevens thinks he's making, the detours he takes to disguise the fact that he's really following another course, and the stops, starts, hesitations by which he exposes his own duplicity to the reader, even as he himself remains deceived. In Ishiguro's novel the real story is a journey of the mind.

Stevens's excursion into the past is not only a personal journey, however; it is also a journey into the history of England. This is not simply a matter of investigating the "facts" of English history. Like Ishiguro's so-called Japanese novels, *Remains* communicates a larger interest in the relationship between personal identity and national consciousness, the relationship between individual and collective memory, and the ways in which those relationships are represented in historical narrative. This novel also voices a specific concern with how the past of Ishiguro's adopted country has been imagined, or constructed, in the writing of English history and literature. Ishiguro's *Remains*, as we shall see, implies that this literary and historical tradition has been a major vehicle of a national consciousness that requires drastic reform. Further, it is in exploring the relationship between national consciousness and personal consciousness that Ishiguro finds a way to express both his interest in universal human themes and his engagement with equally pressing, though more local, problems of English politics and English literary form.

STYLE, FORM, AND IRONY

In *Remains*, as in all of Ishiguro's novels, the primary source of interest is not what happens, but what the narrator says and why he says it. Talk is the major event in all of Ishiguro's works, and one of the first impressions given by this novel is that of a sense of verbal release: Stevens speaks (or, to be more precise, writes) like a man who has waited a long time for an opportunity to express himself. Now that he has his chance, Stevens hardly indulges in an uncontrolled flow of discourse; on the contrary, his monologue is controlled, decorous, restrained. Stevens is as methodical when he speaks as when he performs his duties as a butler. His sentences are carefully and solidly constructed (his slips are few, and when they come they are always revealing); his diction is simple, ordinary, and precise (perhaps too precise). There is a kind of over-formality to Stevens's language — a feature shared, as one reviewer has noted, by all of Ishiguro's narrators — which suggests that something else is being said beneath its carefully polished surface, or at least that the narrator is straining to limit the range of his discourse, to frame it in such a way that things he doesn't want the reader to see are kept out of sight. In Stevens's case, this language is pure "butlerspeak," as David Lodge has called it — a language that in itself "has no literary merit whatsoever [...] completely lacking in wit, sensuousness and originality." Stevens holds our attention, however, because his language repeatedly confesses its own shortcomings as a means of telling his story.

The stiffness of Stevens's speech exhibits itself most visibly in his benighted disquisitions on "bantering," his term for the lighthearted conversation in which his American employer, Mr. Farraday, tries to engage him. The first of these moments occurs in the Prologue, when Farraday teases Stevens about his plans for visiting Miss Kenton, the romantic point of which is quickly perceived by the commonsensical Farraday but denied (in the diary, though not in person) by the flustered Stevens. Stevens makes a futile attempt to hide his embarrassment from the reader by attributing it to unfamiliarity with Farraday's easygoing ways, with which (he says) he must come to terms in order to please his new employer. Thus Stevens represents bantering as a new professional duty that he must master if he is to maintain the standards of perfection to which he holds himself. His explanation of Farraday's penchant for bantering—that Farraday is an American—is unpersuasive, and hardly excuses his own miserable failure to respond in kind. Jokingly asked by Farraday if he was responsible for a certain "crowing noise" that a pair of passing gypsies had made earlier in the day, Stevens tries to live up to the stereotype of the English butler, for which his employer is paying good money, by "thinking of some witty reply":

"More like swallows than crows, I would have said, sir. From the migratory aspect." And I followed this with a suitably modest smile to indicate without ambiguity that I had made a witticism, since I did not wish Mr Farraday to restrain any spontaneous mirth he felt out of a misplaced respectfulness.

Mr Farraday, however, simply looked up at me and said: "I beg your pardon, Stevens?" (pp. 16–17)

This is desperate stuff, and the same has to be said of Stevens's attempts to fend off Farraday's bantering, especially when it touches, as it often does, on the very sexual material that he wants to avoid ("Maybe you could take her out to one of those stables around Mr Morgan's farm. Keep her entertained in all that hay" [p. 15]). Stevens claims to be shocked by such remarks, but tries to defuse them by observing that perhaps they were merely intended as bantering.

Stevens employs the same tactics when describing the two conversations that frame his journey to the West Country. Each of these incidents features another solitary old man, whom Stevens finds seated on a bench. "Perhaps it is indeed time I began to look at this whole matter of bantering more enthusiastically," Stevens observes in his plodding fashion, at the end of the second of these encounters, which occurs on the pier at Weymouth. "After all, when one thinks about it, it is not such a foolish thing to indulge in—particularly if it is the case that in bantering lies the key to human warmth." Yet again, Stevens rationalizes away the human factor and rephrases the issue as a professional matter: "It occurs to me, furthermore, that bantering is hardly an unreasonable duty for an employer to expect a professional to perform" (p. 245). In his very last words, Stevens announces that he will practice his bantering skills in order to surprise Farraday on his return to Darlington Hall. That Stevens's narrative is framed by such matching incidents indicates how deeply hemmed-in he is by his own inflexibility and lack of spontaneity.

One reviewer has complained that it is impossible to take such a self-deluded narrator seriously; surely, the argument goes, no reader is going to be fooled by Stevens's excuses and rationalizations. But such objections miss the point; Ishiguro doesn't expect his readers to be fooled, precisely because at some level Stevens himself isn't fooled either. Stevens has barely begun his narrative before he has given us all the information we need in order to draw conclusions at odds with his own. His refusal to accept these conclusions tells us not that he is stupid but that he is stubborn, or wilfully blind to the truth; indeed, the implication is that his blindness stems from an inability to confront the truth about himself. Hence Stevens's tendency to impart information—such as the tears that stream down his face as he serves the port on the night of his father's death—that belies the stiff upper lip he tries to maintain throughout his narrative. As Ishiguro has explained to Graham Swift: "He ends up saying the sorts of things he does because somewhere deep down he knows which things he has to avoid. He is intelligent enough, in the true sense of the word, to perceive the danger areas, and this controls how his narrative goes."

In *Remains* Ishiguro devises a style that tells the reader something is wrong even as the narrator claims the opposite. In this sense, the language of this novel is analogous to the "translationese" (as Ishiguro has called it) of his two previous books—the first of which, *A Pale View of Hills*, is told by Etsuko, a Japanese exile living in England, and the second, *An Artist of the Floating World*, by Masuji Ono, a Japanese narrator who is supposed to be speaking in Japanese. In the first case, Etsuko's language should strike the English reader as slightly foreign, because English is her second language; in the second case, Ono's narration should hit a similarly false note, because it is a "pseudotranslation," an English translation of an imaginary Japanese text. In similar fashion, Stevens's narration often reads like a stilted English translation of a foreign language by someone with a technical grasp of the forms of English speech but little control over its meaning. Hence the frequency with which Stevens seems to mean something different from what he actually says—an effect that registers an inner turmoil he cannot afford to confront head-on. Appearing always to stand at an ironic distance from its real meaning, Stevens's language indirectly reveals a fracture in his psyche and in his soul. As the narrative proceeds and the ironic gap between meaning and intention widens, we are likely to wonder less at Stevens's stupidity than at the severity of the wound. And as our bafflement increases, we may find ourselves contemplating the mounting cost of Stevens's persistence in speaking the "language of self-deception and self-protection," as Ishiguro put it in an interview with Gregory Mason (1989). It is only late in the day that Stevens recognizes, fleetingly, what the reader has already guessed: this is also the language of broken hearts.

Irony, of course, is the major narrative device that Ishiguro employs in *Remains* to convey depths of meaning that the narrator misses, evades, or attempts to conceal. Irony is not only the product of Ishiguro's style, however; it is communicated by various narrative techniques and also, perhaps most obviously, by his choice of the diary form as the means of relating his tale. The diary has had a long and intriguing history as a literary form, dating back to the Renaissance in the West and the tenth century in Japan, and including among its most famous English exponents the likes of Samuel Pepys, James Boswell, and Virginia Woolf. It has also been deployed to powerful effect in numerous works of European fiction, beginning with Daniel Defoe in *Robinson Crusoe* (1719) and Johann Wolfgang von Goethe in *The Sorrows of Young Werther* (1774), and intensifying in the nineteenth and twentieth centuries, which produced such masterpieces of diary fiction as Gogol's "The Diary of a Madman" (1835), Turgenev's *Diary of a Superfluous Man* (1850), and Sartre's *Nausea* (1938), as well as the modern Japanese diary novels of Ibuse and Tanizaki. Ishiguro, whose contribution to this history comprises not only *Remains* but also the early story "Getting Poisoned" and two other novels, *An Artist of the Floating World* and *When We Were Orphans*, offers some useful insights into the uses of the diary form in his interview with Mason: "Technically, the advantage of the diary narrative is that each entry can be written from a different emotional position. What he [Ono, the narrator of *Artist*] writes in October 1948 is actually written out of a different set of assumptions than the pieces that are written later on." The cumulative effect of several different entries is that they relativize each other; each one has the potential to cast the others in an ironic light. The diary form, moreover, is able to accommodate an unusually wide range of emotional and psychological states, and so permits novelists to indicate the breadth and depth of their characters in ways that open up large vistas of irony. As Lorna Martens puts it in her invaluable study, *The Diary Novel* (1985), a diarist "can be as inconsistent as he wishes." Even though Stevens's entries are written over a period of days rather than several years, Ishiguro manages to exploit all of these sources of irony in *Remains*. Indeed, one effect of this compressed time-frame is to render the changes in the narrator's emotional position all the more startling, for they confront us with the inner turbulence that lies behind the mask of unflappable professional servant.

In *Remains* there are two crucial (and interrelated) incidents that indicate just such a change of perspective on the part of the narrator, and that highlight his status as the object of dramatic irony. The first incident concerns Stevens's treatment of Miss Kenton on an occasion that he himself identifies as a "turning point" in his life (p. 175). Stevens recalls that when he gave Miss Kenton a letter informing her of the death of her aunt, he initially forgot to offer his condolences, and that he then hesitated to "make good [his] omission," because this would have meant intruding on her grief (he surmises that "it was not impossible that Miss Kenton, at that very moment, and only a few feet from me, was actually crying" [p. 176]). Stevens dwells on this supposedly thoughtful hesitation to distract the reader from his insensitivity in the previous scene, and presumably it is for the same reason that he adds: "But eventually I judged it best to await another opportunity to express my sympathy and went on my way" (p. 177). Immediately, however, Stevens undercuts himself by remarking that when he saw Miss Kenton later in the day, he vented his dissatisfaction with the two new maidservants under her supervision. Something else is odd about Stevens's account of this episode, too: why should he suspect Miss Kenton of being grief-stricken by her aunt's death, when he has just noted with approval the "composed" manner in which she received the news (p. 176)? The answer, which entails an arresting confession of his own unreliability as a narrator, comes forty-odd pages afterward, as Stevens waits for Miss Kenton (or Mrs. Benn, as she is now called) in the dining room of the hotel in Little Compton, Cornwall—their first meeting since her departure from Darlington Hall. Stevens says that he has been preoccupied all morning by a "fragment of memory [. . .] a recollection of standing alone in the back corridor before the closed door of Miss Kenton's parlour" (p. 212), which—in a gesture that is typical of Ishiguro's narrators— he now sees he has attached to the wrong episode. Stevens had stood outside Miss Kenton's door on a different occasion altogether— that is, after his clumsy rejection of her timorous but unmistakable offer of love. It is in recognizing how he missed this opportunity that Stevens is able to put this dislocated "fragment" in what feels like its proper place. The pathos of this moment of dim self-recognition is only deepened when Miss Kenton appears at the hotel and confirms that she, too, has often looked back and won-dered what would have happened if they had acted differently at that crucial moment in their lives—at which Stevens realizes his "heart was breaking" (p. 239).

In Stevens's mind, the night when he rejected Miss Kenton's advances is inextricably connected with his memory of one of Lord Darlington's most important conferences, which brought together the British Prime Minister, the Foreign Secretary, and Ribbentrop, Hitler's Foreign Minister and (from 1936 to 1938) Ambassador to Britain. It is typical of Stevens that he brushes off Miss Kenton by insisting that he must attend to his duties because "events of global significance are taking place in this house at this very moment" (to which Miss Kenton's caustic and telling reply is, "When are they not, Mr Stevens?" [p. 218]). The point is clear: Stevens's commit-ment to professional duties repeatedly serves as an excuse for evad-ing the deeper emotional issues of his life. The nature of this evasion also prepares us for the second significant change of perspective on Stevens's part—a change that concerns his attitude toward his employer. Stevens, as we have noted, is utterly devoted to Lord Darlington, and refuses to doubt him even when young Cardinal states quite plainly that he has become the "pawn" of the Nazis (p. 222): "I'm sorry, sir, but I have to say that I have every trust in his lordship's good judgement" (p. 225). By the closing scene on Weymouth pier, this trust has evaporated, taking with it both Stevens's idealized image of Lord Darlington and his own self-respect:

Lord Darlington wasn't a bad man. He wasn't a bad man at all. And at least he had the privilege of being able to say at the end of his life that he made his own mistakes. His lordship was a courageous man. He chose a certain path in life, it proved to be a misguided one, but there, he chose it, he can say that at least. As for myself, I cannot even claim that. You see, I *trusted*. I trusted in his lordship's wisdom. All those years I served him, I trusted I was doing something worthwhile. I can't even say I made my own mistakes. Really—one has to ask oneself—what dignity is there in that? (p. 243)

Now Stevens sees that in giving Lord Darlington his unquestioning devotion, he has condemned himself to a fate even worse than his master's, for in leading a merely vicarious existence he has become the pawn of a pawn. At this moment of partial self-recognition, Stevens is forced to accept that the concept on which he has founded his entire life—dignity—is hollow.

It is worth noting that the issue here is not, as some readers think, unreliable narration—or not, at least, what we usually mean by this term. Wayne Booth, in *The Rhetoric of Fiction* (1961; revised 1983), uses the phrase "unreliable narration" to describe the ways in which an author goes behind the narrator's back to make the reader doubt the narrator's account of events. David Lodge illustrates this concept in *The Art of Fiction* (1992) by discussing Ishiguro's *Remains*, and, on the face of it, has good reason for doing so, if only because unreliable narration is a typical feature of diary fiction (a sub-genre that often exploits the tension between fiction and reality). As other critics have pointed out, however, Ishiguro seems more interested in questioning the concept of unreliable narration than in demonstrating it. In *Remains*, as we have seen, Stevens himself acknowledges his unreliability as a narrator; at one point he even says that he may have attributed to Miss Kenton words actually spoken by Lord Darlington (p. 60). Stevens is, if anything, reliably unreliable, and sometimes he seems determined not to let us forget it. He is also generous with information that permits us to construct an interpretation of his life that is deeply at odds with his own — information that enables us to reach a clearer understanding of his life than he himself ever attains. But this is not simply a question of differences of interpretation; Ishiguro renders uncertain the fictional reality that is the subject of interpretation. When Stevens doubts whether he has attributed reported speech to the correct speaker, we are likely to question the reliability of his "facts" as well as his interpretation of them. Instead of encouraging us to ask, "what happened?," *Remains* invites us to pay attention to the "way of happening" (in Auden's memorable phrase) that is embodied in Stevens's narration.

What Stevens's moments of partial self-recognition do produce, however, is a sharply ironic attitude in the reader, who is thus brought to review with deep skepticism those episodes, in particular, in which Stevens attempts to establish his own superior knowledge. A nice example of this is the tale of the housemaid Lisa, whom Miss Kenton hires against Stevens's advice only to see her run away (as Stevens claims he predicted) with a footman. Ishiguro complicates the irony, however, by declining entirely to close it. While Stevens appears to glimpse something of the truth about himself, that glimpse is fleeting; by ending in renewed pursuit of the old red herring of bantering, he more or less admits that having acquired a modicum of self-knowledge, he has no idea what to do with it. Having shown how wrong events have proved him to be, Stevens shuts down again, as if confessing his own helplessness. If the conclusion of his tale brings him closer to the reader, a certain chilly distance is maintained, leaving us to wonder how much he has changed—an irony at the expense of the more expected ironies that are supposed to result from the changes in "emotional position" which are often recorded in diaries.

In this sense, Ishiguro's use of the diary form corresponds fairly closely to the way James Joyce employs it at the end of *A Portrait of the Artist as a Young Man* (1916), where Stephen Dedalus's first-person account indicates not only the possibility that he shall later develop into a true artist but also the contrary possibility that he is already circling back toward his origins. Joyce implies that the hero may decline, or prove unable, to follow the path of self-development for which the flexible, improvisational form of the diary seems to be the perfect literary vehicle. In *Remains* Ishiguro pursues this idea to a grimly logical conclusion by making his narrator an older man whose career confirms the pessimistic overtones of Joyce's text while suppressing its more optimistic ones. The result, in Ishiguro's novel as in Joyce's, is a hero who ends poised before a gulf of irony that isolates him from author and reader, and that frustrates the freedom apparently allowed by his chosen narrative form.

The fictional diary of *Remains* affirms this ironic distance between narrator and reader by highlighting how the same words may perform two different functions at one stroke. Read as Stevens's utterance, the narration seems designed to suppress meanings that he fails to recognize, or can't face; read as Ishiguro's novel, those words disclose such meanings and the ways in which Stevens has distorted them. The narrative is like a mirror that shows us Stevens as he sees himself, or as he wants us to see him, but that also enables us to picture him quite differently. Stevens's narration, in other words, implies two different readers at the same time: first, the sympathetic, imaginary "you," to whom Stevens ostensibly addresses his remarks as if he were speaking, like T. S. Eliot's Prufrock, to a close associate; second, the reader of the novel, of whom Stevens is inevitably unaware, but whose distance from him, while accentuated by the barrier of print, is mitigated by the sympathy generated by his tale. The polish and transparency of Ishiguro's style serves to heighten both the differences between these two readings and the points at which they overlap. In the process, this style illuminates the degree to which Stevens sees the truth about himself and the degree to which he misses it; it offers us enlightenment, in other words, but also a clear view of enlightenment's failure. For in the end Stevens remains in the dark, a state that is clarified by our apprehension of the gulf of understanding that separates us from him. Yet that clarification only goes so far; ultimately, Stevens's obdurate blindness is inexplicable, unfathomable. Having shown us everything we need to imagine a different portrait from the one he wants us to see, why does he persist in pointing to the latter version of himself as the true one? This is the deeper mystery of Stevens's character, one that, at the end of the day, leaves the reader in the dark as well.

CHARACTER: DIGNITY AND REPRESSION

Commenting in an interview (1991) on the stylistic similarities between his first two novels, Ishiguro observed that *The Remains of the Day* represents an attempt to work out the implications of his style at a thematic level. What has already begun to emerge from our discussion is that this novel's themes are inseparable from the issue of the narrator's character; indeed, character itself is a major theme. By allowing us to glimpse the mystery at the heart of Stevens's character, Ishiguro explores the implications of a style of understatement and indirection that had come to feel like his "natural voice." It is in Stevens that problems of style and theme meet, and this novel is quite remarkable for its sensitivity to the intersection of questions of literary form with problems of social form that takes place in the representation of a character in a work of fiction. Ishiguro's *Remains* requires special alertness, on the reader's part, to the ways in which issues of characterization (the literary methods or techniques that an author employs to represent his characters) dovetail with issues of personality (the combination of psychological, emotional, and moral features that define the individual person who is represented).

In a more recent interview (1995), Ishiguro has speculated that the obsessions driving Stevens's narrative in *Remains*—the desire to control his life, the fear of losing control, and the consequent stifling of emotion—may well be fictional versions of his own preoccupations as a writer. It is the writer's own character, perhaps, that is represented in this novel. Hence the need to work out the implications of his narrative style in a rather different fashion in his next novel, *The Unconsoled*: "Some of the things I'd gone through in writing the book, looking at the benefits and costs of being so controlled in all aspects of your life, as the butler is, led me to think I should write about more messy areas of myself." But, as Ishiguro has emphasized elsewhere, this conflict between control and chaos is not just a writer's preoccupation; it is a common element of ordinary human experience. In his efforts to control those elements— especially sex and politics—that threaten his life with disorder, the butler-narrator of *Remains* distinguishes himself an Everyman figure. Stevens's Prufrockian rationalizations and self-deceptions, his constant reordering of the past in the very act of recalling it (a true remembering), merely confirm his extraordinary ordinariness. This is a quality that Stevens shares with other Ishiguro narrators, such as Etsuko, Ono, and, most recently, Christopher Banks of *When We Were Orphans*. In those novels as in this, the contours and dimensions of the narrative, its obsessions, repetitions, and ironic reversals, give expressive shape to what are, in the end, utterly normal ways of thinking and feeling. What they show us is the hearts and minds of entirely ordinary characters, who suffer because they lack deep insight into their lives.

Ordinariness, in the case of Stevens, takes the particular form of an obsession with "dignity." This term crops up frequently in all of Ishiguro's first three novels, and it helps to explain the way the memories of his narrators work. In *A Pale View of Hills* Etsuko, wracked by guilt after her first daughter's suicide, feels the "need to arrange her memories in a way that allows her to salvage some dignity," as Ishiguro told Gregory Mason; in a different interview (1987) he made the same point about Masuji Ono, the once prestigious but now out-of-favor Japanese artist who narrates *An Artist of the Floating World*. Stevens differs from those narrators, however, by engaging in an ultimately vain pursuit of the meaning of dignity. On the face of it, Stevens is bent on defining the term in order to clarify his "professional values" (p. 35), but clearly he is obsessed with it because he believes it holds the key to his whole life. Therein, of course, lies Stevens's problem: he identifies himself so completely with his professional role that without it he would be nothing.

The pretext for Stevens's inquiry into the meaning of dignity is his attempt to answer the question, "*what* is a great butler?" (p. 31). For an answer to this question, Stevens turns to the fictitious Hayes Society, which asserts in the pages of the *Quarterly for the Gentleman's Gentleman* that a butler of "the very first rank" is distinguished by a "dignity in keeping with his position" (p. 33). As Stevens observes, this begs the question, "of what is 'dignity' comprised?" Dissatisfied with the venerable Mr. Graham's claim that dignity was "like a woman's beauty" — "something one possessed or did not by a fluke of nature," and therefore beyond analysis — Stevens contends that it may be acquired "over many years of self-training and the careful absorbing of experience" (p. 33). Still the concept eludes definition, forcing Stevens to abandon analysis for illustration and narrative — which brings him to his father's tale of the British butler in India, who, without turning a hair, dispatched a tiger in the dining room, having assured his employer that by the time dinner is served "there will be no discernible traces left of the recent occurrence" (p. 36). After embellishing this story with testimony to his father's own qualities as a butler in a great house, Stevens explains that dignity "has to do crucially with a butler's ability not to abandon the professional being he inhabits":

Lesser butlers will abandon their professional being for the private one at the least provocation. For such persons, being a butler is like playing some pantomime role; a small push, a slight stumble, and the facade will drop off to reveal the actor underneath. The great butlers are great by virtue of their ability to inhabit their professional role and inhabit it to the utmost; they will not be shaken out by external events, however surprising, alarming, or vexing. They wear their professionalism as a decent gentleman will wear his suit: he will not let ruffians or circumstance tear it off him in the public gaze; he will discard it when, and only when, he wills to do so, and this will invariably be when he is entirely alone. (pp. 42–43)

Stevens himself exemplifies an almost infinite capacity for this quality in various incidents recalled during his narrative, most notably in his accounts of Lord Darlington's two great conferences. During the first of these events, Stevens says, he continued to perform his butler's duties even while in another room his father (now his under-butler) lay dying. Stevens did exactly the same thing on the second such occasion, when Miss Kenton, in a final attempt to

arouse his dormant emotions, announced that she had accepted Mr
Benn's proposal of marriage. As Brian Shaffer explains in *Understanding Kazuo Ishiguro* (1998), the clothing metaphors that Stevens uses to describe his devotion to professional duty serves only to
cloak his emotional and sexual repression. Paradoxically, this strategy merely draws attention to the way he wears these clothes — that
is, to the very mechanisms of repression.

Ishiguro has claimed, somewhat misleadingly, that Stevens, as
the "perfect butler," is a metaphor "for someone who is trying to
actually erase the emotional part of him that may be dangerous and
that could really hurt him in his professional area." A careful reading of *Remains* suggests that the opposite is closer to the truth:
Stevens's preoccupation with professional dignity, which is reflected
in his efforts to maintain a controlled and reserved narratorial de-
meanor, serves to repress personal feeling. This repression manifests
itself in three major ways. First, and most obviously, it betrays itself
in Stevens's relationship with Miss Kenton, the romantic nature of
which he never admits to himself until it is too late. Second,
Stevens's repression emerges in his inability to offer even conventional expressions of filial tenderness toward his father, to whom he
refers almost always in the third person, even when addressing him
directly. The third form taken by Stevens's repression is a peculiarly
outmoded and self-effacing political attitude, which is deeply connected (as we shall see) to the problem of father-son relations. All
of these manifestations of repression insinuate that Stevens's butlering finally amounts to nothing but technique — that it is style without substance, and thus, in an important sense, no style at all.
Remains allows the reader to count the emotional and psychological
cost of the dignified style for a man who is consumed by his
professional role.

Stevens employs the concept of "dignity" to rationalize his ab-
surd behavior during a crucial scene with Miss Kenton, which

underlines the theme of sexual repression and, not surprisingly, precipitates a crisis in their relationship. The incident, as Stevens recalls it, goes like this: One evening he was sitting in the pantry ("a crucial office," which he compares with "a general's headquarters during a battle" [p. 165]), taking advantage of a rare hour off duty to read a book, when Miss Kenton enters and insists on seeing what he's reading. Stevens assumes all sorts of ridiculous postures, "clutching" the book "to [his] person" and rising defensively to his feet, before Miss Kenton takes it from him—an action that he characterizes as a kind of sexual violation, and that culminates in a farcical, but nonetheless revealing, deflation:

She reached forward and began gently to release the volume from my grasp. I judged it best to look away while she did so, but with her person positioned so closely, this could only be achieved by my twisting my head away at a somewhat unnatural angle. Miss Kenton continued very gently to prise the book away, practically one finger at a time. The process seemed to take a very long time—throughout which I managed to maintain my posture—until finally I heard her say:

"Good gracious, Mr. Stevens, it isn't anything so scandalous at all. Simply a sentimental love story." (p. 167)

Deciding that he can't tolerate any more, Stevens dismisses Miss Kenton from his sanctuary, and then makes a futile attempt to explain away her discovery by claiming that he was reading this book merely to improve his "command of the English language" (p. 167). Miss Kenton's intrusion is to be resented, in other words, not as the sexual advance that it clearly is, but as an interruption of his professional activities. To be sure, Stevens avers, Miss Kenton's conduct signals a departure from the principle of dignity that governs their professional lives. Stevens hammers the point home by reiterating his earlier definition of dignity, and concludes: "You will appreciate then that in the event of Miss Kenton bursting in at a time when I had presumed, not unreasonably, that I was to be alone, it came to be a crucial matter of principle, a matter indeed of dignity, that I did not appear in anything less than my full and proper role" (p. 169). Stevens, who later makes explicit what is implicit here by telling Dr. Carlisle that dignity "comes down to not removing one's clothing in public" (p. 210), responds to Miss Kenton's invasion of his private domain by declaring that their relationship has reached an "inappropriate footing," and by resolving to reestablish it "on a more proper basis" (p. 169). In this way Stevens closes off the possibility of a love story that Miss Kenton has tried so hard to keep open, leading one to conclude that he himself is a closed book. But however hard Stevens tries to present himself in this fashion, it's easy to read between the lines.

The emotional repression that manifests itself in Stevens's relationship with his father is inextricable from his political repression, and it is moreover intertwined with his ongoing attempt to define dignity. As we have seen, it is to his father that Stevens turns when attempting to define dignity in the first place, citing his career as a butler and his anecdotes about other butlers to illustrate his idea of professional perfection. Stevens asserts that his father embodies dignity all the more effectively for his very lack of "various attributes one may normally expect in a great butler [. . .] such as good accent and command of language, general knowledge on wide-ranging topics such as falconing or newt-mating"—superficial qualities that the uninitiated sometimes mistake for true dignity, but that are really no more than "icing on the cake" (p. 34). Yet this account of a butler's dignity does not square with every aspect of Stevens's own conduct. Although he excuses his father's imperfect "command of language" as inessential to the art of butlering, Stevens (as we have noted) gives the need to improve his own language as his reason for reading sentimental romances. While this statement is intended to conceal Stevens's sexual emotions, it also reveals a professional ambition to surpass the standards set by his father. Hence, perhaps, the emotional distance between father and son that emerges in their verbal exchanges, during which Stevens refers to his father in the third person, while the latter's contributions are typically delivered in a strikingly brusque, and apparently unfeeling, tone of voice. If Stevens hadn't told us that the under-butler was his father, we could be forgiven for thinking of their relationship as an exclusively professional affair. Only in their very last conversation, on the night of Lord Darlington's first great conference, do father and son break out of their professional roles to speak in tones approaching filial intimacy:

He went on looking at his hands for a moment. Then he said slowly: "I hope I've been a good father to you."

I laughed a little and said: "I'm so glad you're feeling better now."

"I'm proud of you. A good son. I hope I've been a good father to you. I suppose I haven't."

"I'm afraid we're extremely busy now, but we can talk again in the morning."

My father was still looking at his hands as though he were faintly irritated by them.

"I'm so glad you're feeling better now," I said again and took my leave. (p. 97)

For once, the two Stevenses employ first- and second-person forms of address. But even now the narrator evades his father's attempt to bridge the emotional hiatus that divides them.

Stevens's awkward relationship with his father is symptomatic of a more general sense of familial displacement, and a corresponding feeling of emotional deprivation, which may lie at the root of his character. If he finds it hard to express his feelings about his father, Stevens never mentions his mother. This is another clear sign of repression, one that is perhaps related to his inability to admit his emotional dependence on Miss Kenton. We also learn that Stevens's elder brother and only sibling, Leonard, was killed in the Boer War (1899–1902). One might expect such a loss to reinforce the bond between father and surviving son, but the opposite seems to be the case; if anything, Stevens senior seems to have encouraged his butler-son to sacrifice everything to professional duty. It's possible that Leonard died in South Africa in response to a similar paternal injunction, and that Stevens himself is congratulated on being a "good son" only because he is, in his own way, following in Leonard's footsteps. Stevens reinforces this idea by recalling that his brother was a needless casualty in an infamously "un-British" attack on Boer civilians, a fate that prefigures his own futile devotion to the Nazi sympathizer, Lord Darlington (p. 40).

Leonard's fate clarifies another important aspect of Stevens's repression, his position in the British political system, which is closely tied to the problematic dynamics of the Stevens family. In their different ways, both brothers have been victims of a lingering feudalism in British society, which solely on grounds of heredity grants authority to the likes of Lord Darlington, who turns out to be, at best, naive or, at worst, treacherous. Stevens's eagerness to accept such authority appears to derive from his father, as he intimates by recounting an episode from his father's years as the butler of Loughborough Hall. When the ex-general responsible for Leonard's death descended on Loughborough Hall in his new guise as businessman, and did so without bringing a valet, Stevens's father volunteered to attend on him, even though his employer, realizing the difficulty of the situation, had given him permission to be absent for the entire visit. This emotional masochism and the political quietism it entails are inherited by Stevens, who cites this incident as an example of his father's dignity. Thus, when Miss Kenton announces that his father has died, Stevens insists on continuing with his professional duties, claiming that, "father would have wished me to carry on just now," and adding: "To do otherwise, I feel, would be to let him down" (p. 106). The ambiguity of Stevens's syntax — by "him," does he mean his father, or Lord Darlington, whose conference is in mid-flow? — suggests not only that he has learned his father's lesson all too well, but also that his experience in Lord Darlington's employ may have reinforced it, so that the call of professional duty inevitably drowns the sounds of a personal emotional crisis. Ishiguro implies that Stevens has so fully imbibed the values of service, or political servility, that it is impossible for him to respond to such a crisis. In other words, if Stevens's emotional repression has contributed to his political repression, it is equally plausible to ask if his political repression hasn't intensified his emotional repression.

Ishiguro develops the intricate connections between father-son relations and class relations by hinting that Lord Darlington has displaced Stevens senior from his natural place in his son's affections — that Lord Darlington has assumed the role, in effect, of a surrogate-father. Stevens points to this possibility in his repeated expressions of admiration for his employer, which stand in stark contrast to the awkwardness of his relationship with his biological father. This displacement of biological by social or political father is underscored by the respective positions of the characters in the British class system: as lord of the manor, Lord Darlington holds an unassailable position of political dominance that makes him a kind of father-figure to his servants. In the world of Darlington Hall, father-son relations — indeed all interpersonal attachments — are subordinate to the feudal bond between master and servant. For this system to operate smoothly, of course, those who occupy servile roles must give their consent; Stevens, like his father, is only too willing to do so.

Stevens thoroughly internalizes the master-servant dynamic and, in his dealings with Lord Darlington, plays his servile role to perfection. It is also important to observe, though, that Stevens reverses this dynamic in his relations with the other servants, including his father and Miss Kenton. Stevens's frequently high-handed treatment of Miss Kenton indicates the extent to which he is prepared to allow the political forces that define his professional persona not only to determine his sense of personal identity (he divulges neither his own first name nor hers) but also to dictate the terms on which all of his relationships with other people are conducted. This double-internalization of the master-servant dynamic, and the subsequent division in Stevens's personality, may also account for his ill-disguised pleasure, as well as professed embarrassment, when the villagers at a West Country inn mistake him for Lord Darlington: the part of Stevens that wants to lord it over other people has led him into over-identification with his master. Thus Stevens passively accepts Lord Darlington's word on political matters, even when young Cardinal tells him point-blank that his employer is the dupe of the Nazis; the only defense Stevens offers to explain the dismissal of two Jewish maids is that he was (in a chilling echo of the Nuremberg trials) simply obeying orders. On one occasion Stevens acquiesces in his own humiliation by his master's guests, responding to their offensive questions about the proverbial man in the street with the very confessions of ignorance that they want to hear. In all of this, Stevens shows how he has been reduced to a mechanism, in a fashion reminiscent of another fictional character without a first name, Farrington, the protagonist of Joyce's great story "Counterparts." Farrington is divided between his servile position at work and his patriarchal role in the home, where he turns the tables on his workplace self by bullying his young son; split between the diametrically opposed, yet mutually reinforcing, roles of master and servant, Stevens is, like Farrington, his own counterpart.

To evoke *Dubliners* (1914) is also to bring to mind Joyce's memorable phrase for the spiritual condition of his characters, "moral

paralysis," which similarly illuminates the frigid interior of Ishiguro's Stevens. At the end of his day, Stevens's repression — psychological, emotional, and political — issues in a sense of moral crisis
closely resembling the atmosphere that pervades Joyce's fictional
world. Like countless members of Joyce's cast, Stevens is unable to
articulate, let alone act out, his real desires. Where do these inhibi-
tions come from? Are they produced by external factors, such as the
British class system? Or do they emanate from the deep heart's
core? Or are they the result of a collaboration between internal and
external forces? Ultimately, having provoked such questions, Ishiguro makes it no easier to answer them than Joyce does. Instead of
explaining his narrator's character, he confronts us with his intrac-
table mysteriousness — with his ability to talk himself into difficulties
that he cannot solve, but only evade.

Stevens's moral paralysis displays itself most powerfully, perhaps,
when his notion of dignity founders during an exchange that occurs
at Moscombe on the third day of his travels. Stevens presents his
interlocutor, Harry Smith, as a stock rustic fool, but Smith's com-
monplace understanding of dignity carries more weight than the
narrator wants to admit. First, Smith rebuts Stevens's claim that
dignity is what distinguishes a gentleman by asserting: "Dignity's
something every man and woman in this country can strive for and
get." Despite Stevens's attempt to muffle it (they were, he remarks,
"rather at cross purposes on this matter"), we may hear in Smith's
egalitarian definition of dignity an ironic echo of the narrator's own
earlier attempt to explain the term. By his persistence, meanwhile,
Smith reveals the falseness of Stevens's position: "That's what we
fought Hitler for, after all. If Hitler had had things his way, we'd
just be slaves now. The whole world would be a few masters and
millions upon millions of slaves. And I don't need to remind anyone
here, there's no dignity to be had in being a slave" (p. 186). Stevens
doesn't comment directly on this pronouncement, but the implica-

tion is clear: through his lifelong loyalty to Lord Darlington, Stevens has willingly enslaved himself to a Nazi appeaser, and thus has helped, if only indirectly, to further Hitler's cause. For a time, Stevens resists this logic, defending the dignity of his faithful service, and attributing the emergence of a different perspective to the "passage of time":

How can one possibly be held to blame in any sense because, say, the passage of time has shown that Lord Darlington's efforts were misguided, even foolish? Throughout the years I served him, it was he and he alone who weighed up evidence and judged it best to proceed in the way he did, while I simply confined myself, quite properly, to affairs within my own professional realm. And as far as I am concerned, I carried out my duties to the best of my abilities[. . .]. It is hardly my fault if his lordship's life and work have turned out today to look, at best, a sad waste—and it is quite illogical that I should feel any regret or shame on my own account. (p. 201)

Yet even now Stevens's defenses are starting to give way, so that the epiphany of waste and shame on Weymouth pier has an air of inevitability when it finally comes: "I can't even say I made my own mistakes. Really—one has to ask oneself—what dignity is there in that?" (p. 243). As a partial revelation of the narrator's own moral paralysis, this moment rivals the end of another work of diary fiction, Christopher Isherwood's *Goodbye to Berlin* (1939), where the narrator catches a glimpse of his own unaccountably smiling face in the mirror while, outside the confines of his room, Hitler takes control of the city.

In conversation with Graham Swift, Ishiguro described *Remains* as a debate between two different notions of dignity: on one hand, a "professional" theory of dignity, which requires the suppression of emotions, and, on the other hand, the "dignity that democracy gives to ordinary people." Harry Smith, for all his bluster, is the ironically clear-sighted spokesman for the second kind of dignity, while Stevens, the ploddingly precise narrator, mounts an ultimately vain defense of the first kind. Yet Stevens's resistance to the democratic view (which also expresses itself in his awkwardness with his egalitarian American employer, Farraday) is not represented as extraordinary or aberrant behavior; on the contrary, Stevens is Ishiguro's portrait of an utterly ordinary man, who struggles to accept change, even when he seems likely to profit by it. In the same interview Ishiguro characterized the butler as a "good metaphor for the relationship of very ordinary, small people to power," and added: "Most of us aren't given governments to run or coup d'etats to lead. We have to offer up the little services we have perfected to various people: to causes, to employers, to organizations and hope for the best—that we approve of the way it gets used." These sentences sum up Stevens's case perfectly, and they indicate the distance that separates him from the center of history's stage. As we have seen, however, Ishiguro's novel also implies that the major threat to Stevens's dignity may derive less from such external causes as political inequality than from the mystery of his own inner nature. "We think of the key, each in his prison / Thinking of the key, each confirms a prison," Eliot wrote in *The Waste Land* (1922); in *The Remains of the Day* Stevens's story-telling not only describes his own psychological imprisonment, but confirms it.

ENGLAND, WHOSE ENGLAND?

While the primary subject of *Remains* is character—the nature of Stevens's character in particular and the texture of human consciousness in general—the novel also explores social and political themes, including the class system, generational conflict, and relations between the sexes. That these themes began to suggest themselves in our discussion of character illustrates the interdependence, in Ishiguro's fictional universe, of the interior world of consciousness and the public world of human society. In *Remains* character is not internally self-generating; it is informed by a complex interplay between internal and external forces. Yet the social and political themes of Ishiguro's work should not be regarded as merely secondary to questions of character; such themes make significant demands on our attention. This point clarifies itself when we observe how issues of class, sex, and generation combine to indicate a deeper question that vexes Stevens as he circles the question of character: What is England, and what is Englishness? Other questions follow from this: Who decides such matters of nationhood and national character? Who writes the history of England, and from what political point of view? While it would be reductive to read *Remains* as an allegory of modern English political history — the critic Hermione Lee rightly points out that Ishiguro's texts, like their titles, only "hover on the borders of allegory" — the novel forces us to confront such issues. In the process, *Remains* reveals a preoccupation with the role and nature of nationalism that unites all of Ishiguro's writings.

The political dimensions of *Remains* display themselves most obviously, as we have observed, in the representation of the English class system, especially as it emerges in the relationship between Stevens and Lord Darlington. Darlington Hall, moreover, is a miniature version of England itself, and the hierarchical arrangement of social relations inside its walls reflects the state of English society at large. Until Stevens embarks on his trip to the West Country, Darlington Hall is his entire world, as he makes clear by describing his "unease mixed with exhilaration" as he leaves its environs and ventures into the unknown "wilderness" of Berkshire (p. 24). Here Ishiguro indicates the limitations imposed on the likes of Stevens by their social position: political subordination expresses itself in a

sense of geographical confinement. Anticipating the troubled mind-
scape of *The Unconsoled*, this scene also connotes an unremitting
psychological anxiety, which confirms one's suspicion that Stevens
has internalized the master-servant dynamic to the point where it
determines every feature of his consciousness as well as his social
relations. But a simpler point emerges, too: just as Darlington Hall
is the property of Lord Darlington, much of England as a whole
remains in the hands of a feudal aristocracy, whose apparent benig-
nity conceals their blindness to problems of social justice that obtain
in the wider political world. Unlike his master, Stevens has no home
of his own, and in a sense he has no country of his own either—a
point that is underlined by the fact that during his journey to the
West Country he drives his new master's car and wears his old
master's clothes.

Read in terms of the historical development of the English novel,
Stevens's political situation may seem to invite a less gloomy response. One of the most remarkable features of Ishiguro's novel is,
after all, its focus on the consciousness of a servant. As George
Orwell famously complained in an essay on Charles Dickens, English fiction tends to be short on representations of the working
class, who only enter Dickens's novels as "objects of pity or as comic
relief." Or, as the contemporary literary critic Bruce Robbins puts it
in *The Servant's Hand* (1986): "Much has changed between Homer
and Virginia Woolf, but the literary servant has not undergone
proportional changes; servants are the commonplaces of many times
and places. Thus a critic like Northrop Frye can claim, using this
figure as a prime exhibit, that the essential forms of literature are
independent of their social context." When servants did start turning
up in English fiction, it was usually in the conventional literary
guise of the master's instrument, or as a comic figure reminiscent
of Elizabethan and Restoration comedy. Although there have been
some exceptions (the novels of Henry Green, for example), this law

continued to exert itself in the works of one of England's most popular modern comic writers, P. G. Wodehouse, while another, Evelyn Waugh, ruled the working class out of fictional bounds (he declared Green's *Loving* [1945], a novel about servants, "obscene"). In a sense, then, Ishiguro's novel is extraordinary simply because it offers a detailed treatment of servant life from the fictionalized point of view of a servant. Yet where Robbins's rereading of literary tradition seeks out instances of the servant's resistance to political repression, Ishiguro's representation of Stevens's consciousness highlights this repression, in terms of both its social manifestations and its psychological effects. Indeed, one of the most powerful implications of *Remains* is that sexual and political repression are interrelated, for each signifies a desire to control chaos — a desire that expresses itself sexually in Stevens's efforts to control the domestic affairs of Darlington Hall, and politically in Lord Darlington's attraction to Fascism. Together, these forms of repression heighten our apprehension of Stevens's disempowerment.

While resisting the ultimately reductive temptations of allegory, Ishiguro hints at the wider world within which Stevens's little corner of England is to be found by setting his tale at the very moment in history when England's status as an imperial power received its first irreparable shock: July 1956, the month of the Suez crisis. Thus Stevens's subjugation may be read not only as a parable of the English class system but also, perhaps, as a far-off echo of the political oppression against which the Egyptian government protested by nationalizing the Suez Canal. To live in a home that is not one's own, which is the undignified fate of Stevens, seems broadly analogous to the condition of a colonized subject; one might even argue that in representing Stevens's plight Ishiguro indicates how colonialism begins at home. But Ishiguro shows, too, how the nationalist ideology expressed by colonialism and imperialism takes shape in the consciousness of an ordinary person. Ironically and poignantly, this point emerges with special force during Stevens's attempt to define dignity, which he regards as an essentially and exclusively English quality:

Continentals are unable to be butlers because they are as a breed incapable of the emotional restraint which only the English race are capable of. Continentals—and by and large the Celts, as you will no doubt agree—are as a rule unable to control themselves in moments of strong emotion, and are thus unable to maintain a professional demeanour other than in the least challenging of situations.[. . .] [T]hey are like a man who will, at the slightest provocation, tear off his suit and his shirt and run about screaming. In a word, "dignity" is beyond such persons. We English have an important advantage over foreigners in this respect and it is for this reason that when you think of a great butler, he is bound, almost by definition, to be an Englishman. (p. 43)

This naked expression of chauvinist nationalism betrays its own illogicality even in Stevens's syntax, as his attempt to maintain control breaks down (the first sentence closes with an ungainly preposition). The point, of course, is that such ideas are hardly Stevens's own. Stevens has barely ventured beyond the grounds of Darlington Hall, and the only foreigners with whom he has come into contact have been Lord Darlington's guests. The views Stevens voices here have probably been picked up from other sources—primarily his master and perhaps his father, and also books, such as *The Wonder of England* by the fictional Mrs Jane Symons, which Stevens takes with him on his travels. To state the obvious, none of these sources enjoys unimpeachable authority; rather, Ishiguro encourages us to meet their surreptitious nationalism with a skeptical eye.

Remains urges such skepticism in various ways, including Stevens's abortive attempts at exercising the sense of humor that is often associated—both by the English themselves and by their foreign observers—with Englishness. The precise extent to which Stevens, in particular, has absorbed the nationalist ideology of modern England is unfolded in another passage—one that precedes his account of dignity as a distinctively English quality—in which he tries to describe the English landscape. In England, Stevens claims, the land "possesses a quality that the landscapes of other nations, however more superficially dramatic, inevitably fail to possess," a quality "best summed up by the term 'greatness,'" which justifies the name "*Great* Britain":

And yet what precisely is this "greatness"? Just where, or in what, does it lie? [. . .] I would say that it is the very *lack* of obvious drama or spectacle that sets the beauty of our land apart. What is pertinent is the calmness of that beauty, its sense of restraint. It is as though the land knows of its own beauty, of its own greatness, and feels no need to shout it. In comparison, the sorts of sights offered in such places as Africa and America, though undoubtedly very exciting, would, I am sure, strike the objective viewer as inferior on account of their unseemly demonstrativeness. (pp. 28–29)

At the very beginning of this passage, Stevens's choice of the word "nations" (rather than "countries") illustrates the questionable tendency to equate characteristics of the land with those of its inhabitants; the sentences that follow reinforce this equation by attributing the human capacity for thinking and feeling to the land. The land itself, in other words, is supposed to contain the roots of English national consciousness. Yet again, however, Stevens's contentions derive not from personal observation, let alone objective knowledge, but from books—encyclopedias and *National Geographic Magazine*, to which he refers a few lines earlier. Stevens's claims about the world, and about the nations into which it has been divided, are guided not by reality but by edited representations of reality; his unconscious nationalism is the product of various fictions, not verifiable truths.

A brief comparison with a passage from A *Pale View of Hills*, Ishiguro's first novel, quickly disabuses one of Stevens's theory of Englishness. At the beginning of Part Two the narrator, Etsuko, remarks: "On clearer days, I could see far beyond the trees on the opposite bank of the river, a pale outline of hills visible against the clouds. It was not an unpleasant view, and on occasions it brought me a rare sense of relief from the emptiness of those long afternoons I spent in that apartment" (p. 99). There is nothing dramatic or spectacular about this landscape either; it, too, is distinguished by its "very lack of obvious drama or spectacle" (to borrow the words Stevens employs in *Remains* to characterize the English landscape). Yet the landscape described here is not English but Japanese: Etsuko is recalling a long hot summer in postwar Nagasaki. The point is that, lifted from its context, the Japanese landscape remembered by Etsuko might be mistaken quite easily for the English landscape that Stevens eulogizes in *Remains*.

Some readers have pointed to such correspondences between Ishiguro's Japan and England in order to suggest, like Salman Rushdie, that the two nations "may not be so very unlike one another." At some level this contention is hard to deny. One obvious connection occurs at the level of language, the "translationese," as Ishiguro calls it, spoken by his Japanese and English narrators alike. Like Etsuko and Ono, Stevens speaks a language of "silence and elusion," in the words of the sociologist Peter N. Dale, whose trenchant critique of the "myth of Japanese uniqueness" not only includes some illuminating comparisons with certain clichés about English reticence, but also provides an inadvertent gloss on the narrator of *Remains* (Dale's phrase, "the dumb language of the intimidated psyche" captures Stevens's plight perfectly). Such critics as Hermione Lee and Anthony Thwaite, moreover, have observed that Stevens recalls the traditional Japanese figure of the *ronin*, a faithful servant who no longer has a master, and that the preoccupation with dignity in all of Ishiguro's first three novels suggests a deep resemblance between English and Japanese culture. In this context it is also worth noting the similarity between Stevens's relationship to Lord Darlington and the master-pupil relationship that occupies a central role in Japanese society, a point that emerges in *An Artist of the Floating World*, as well as in Soseki's famous novel *Kokoro* (1914): both English and Japanese society seem to require a tradition of service that doubles as a form of patriotic nationalism. But it is wrong to conclude from such evidence that *Remains* is simply a Japanese novel in disguise (as Lee argues), or that it warns us to be "less Japanese" (as Gabriele Annan claims). The real point is that in Ishiguro's hands England and Japan become very difficult to tell apart, so that one is bound to regard the nationalism of either country as a matrix of ideological constructions whose claims we should try to resist, if we wish to preserve any sense of individual dignity.

It is also possible to read the correspondences between Ishiguro's representations of Japan and England as signs of a deep-seated concern with universal human themes, accompanied by a desire both to defeat politics in general and to subvert the specific nationalist tendency — typified by Stevens — to foster myths of national or racial superiority. It is worth recalling Ishiguro's warning to Western readers of Kawabata's novels: "Of course, you *will* find characters behaving oddly and obsessively, but this is more likely to be because they are characters in a Kawabata novel, rather than because they are Japanese." The same goes for Ishiguro's Stevens, whose emotional repression might be regarded as a human affliction, rather than as a peculiarly English one, and whose attempt to repair his faltering sense of dignity echoes the similar efforts of Etsuko and Ono in Ishiguro's previous two novels. In Ishiguro's fictional world, dignity is a floating or homeless concept. Unless we respond to Stevens as an individual person, regardless of his nationality, the emotional impact of his tale is diminished.

But in addition to calling for a response to the plight of the suffering individual, Ishiguro's novels invite us to consider how the myth or ideology of nationhood is constructed, or invented, in both fiction and history — and, beyond that, to contemplate the way in which history itself is constructed. This means confronting the element of invention involved in any form of representation, whether literary, historical, or ideological. Ishiguro has insisted (as we noted in Chapter 1) that the Japan depicted in his first two novels is an invented country, the product of memory, speculation, and imagination, and he has made similar claims for his representation of England in *Remains*, describing it as both a "pastiche" and a "mythical England." Contrasting himself with such precursors as Wodehouse, Waugh, and E. M. Forster, Ishiguro asks his reader to recognize the ironic distance between this mythical land and popular idealized images of England. His aim, he has stated, was not to reproduce historical reality (to which, in any case, we do not have straightforward access) but to "rework a particular myth about a certain kind of mythical England [. . .] an England with sleepy, beautiful villages with very polite people and butlers and people taking tea on the lawn." While reminding us that such subversive work is also meant to make a universal appeal, Ishiguro has expressed a strong desire to resist a "nostalgia industry" that is often harmless but whose "Garden of Eden" image of England is sometimes exploited for objectionable political ends: "This can be brought out by the left or right, but usually it is the political right who say England was this beautiful place before the trade unions tried to make it more egalitarian or before the immigrants started to come or before the promiscuous age of the '60s came and ruined everything." Ishiguro observes that tackling and reworking cultural myths — whether those of "beautiful" England or the American West — is one of the most important tasks that modern novelists face. "A nation's myth is the way a country dreams," Ishiguro says, and Stevens's nostalgia for the "mythical England" of the Twenties and Thirties reveals his dreams to be forms of unconscious nationalism.

This imperative to combat the "nostalgia industry" and its unsavory political implications is one of the forces driving Ishiguro's attempt to discover "some territory, somewhere between straight realism and [. . .] out-and-out fabulism" — in other words, to create a narrative form that makes readers aware they are encountering a fictional world that resembles the real one, without ceding too much ground either to a naive realism (which purports to represent the real world as it actually is) or an extreme anti-realism (which makes no pretense at describing a life-like world). One sign of Ishiguro's intentions on this score is his creation of a semi-fictional "England," which approximates closely to historical and geographical reality without conforming to it in all particulars. Darlington Hall, for instance, is not a real place, although it has numerous features that evoke the general description of a stately home and is situated near a real city (Oxford). Similarly, while Stevens's journey takes him to actual places, such as Salisbury, Taunton, and Weymouth, he also visits several invented places: Mortimer's Pond, Moscombe, and Little Compton. These invented places, however, are situated in or near real ones: the first is to be found in Dorset, we are told, the second near Tavistock, Devon, and the last in Cornwall. This mixture of fictional with actual place names is unusual in English fiction, and in American fiction, for that matter: the only major parallels are to be found in the novels of Hardy and Faulkner. Like Ishiguro's England, Hardy's Wessex and Faulkner's Yoknapatawpha are invented regions; while many of their towns and landmarks correspond to real places in (respectively) the English West Country and the American South, and are sometimes given their actual names, their fictional status allows them to be treated as worlds that run parallel to the actual historical world and that follow similar laws, without being held exactly accountable to them. In some ways the connection with Hardy is quite pronounced: Wessex corresponds closely to the geographical terrain that Stevens covers during his journey in *Remains*. In locating Darlington Hall near Oxford (Hardy's Christminster) and concluding the action in Weymouth (which, in the guise of Budmouth, appears more frequently than any other place in Hardy's fiction), Ishiguro calls attention to this correspondence, as if to suggest that his England amounts to a reinvention not only of historical England but also of Hardy's Wessex. Whereas Hardy strived harder and harder to forge direct links between Wessex and the real England, however, Ishiguro continues to insist on a certain distance; in this respect he is closer to Faulkner than to Hardy.

One effect of this strategy in *Remains* is to render transparent the fictionalizing in which Stevens indulges as he recounts the story of his own past and the recent history of England—a story that exemplifies the very nostalgia Ishiguro is calling into question. One is led to feel, perhaps, that Stevens's representation of events corresponds more or less to what we think we know of historical reality, but that somehow it depends too heavily on his fantasies, or illusions, for it to be entirely credible. Ishiguro creates a similar effect in *An Artist of the Floating World*, whose unnamed city several critics have readily identified as Tokyo, but which is intended (as Ishiguro asserts in a 1987 interview) to be a fictional place with the "flexibility of [an] imagined world." Ishiguro's aim in mingling real with invented place-names in *Remains* may have been simply to make this point more explicit—a speculation that is supported by the fact that the Central European city featured in his next novel, *The Unconsoled*, is specified neither by name nor by any set of recognizable features. That Stevens traverses a part of England that has already been fictionalized by Hardy reinforces this possibility.

We shouldn't trust Stevens's version of England, then, because its fictionality is highly conspicuous. Equally unmistakable are the personal motives that drive the narrator's fictionalizing and its latent political content. There is a parallel, as we have seen, between Stevens's desire to quell the threat of sexual anarchy within Darlington Hall and Lord Darlington's Fascistic desire to suppress political anarchy without. Ishiguro's novel hints that the conventions of English story-telling, both fictional and historical, may reinforce such political motives, and that novel-writing and history-writing may even be the preeminent cultural forms in which national consciousness is articulated. Yet *Remains* also insinuates that a subtle reinvention of these narrative conventions may generate a certain political resistance that discloses the means by which the English novel, in particular, has put itself at the service of English nationalism. By exposing Stevens's Englishness as a theatrical persona, an impersonation of a mythical role that conforms to nothing verifiable in England itself (even Stevens's language, we might recall, sounds more like a translation than actual living speech), Ishiguro subverts the nationalist ideology that he parrots at crucial moments in the text. Stevens's inability to fool Dr. Carlisle when attempting to pass himself off as an aristocrat—to play the role of Lord Darlington, in other words—not only lays bare the impermeability of class barriers; it points to the frailty of Stevens's nostalgia-ridden notion of Englishness, and its dependence on the social divisions it is supposed to suppress.

A similar point may be made about the novel itself. *Remains* is not so much an English novel as a "super-English novel" ("*more English than English*," as Ishiguro has put it); it is a novel that mimics the conventions and habits of "Great House" English fiction in order to reveal its blind spots. If it seems unconvincing (as one reviewer has claimed) to find Stevens spending his leisure hours reading in the parlor, this may be less an "error" on Ishiguro's part than a ploy designed to alert us to the shaky foundations of the narrator's representation of English social history. Thus *Remains* gives us what the literary critic Steven Connor has called a double-impersonation, which maintains a constant parallel "between the representation of England and Englishness and its exploration of the possibilities of its own form."

This irreverent mimicry of Englishness and its narrative incarnations is only intensified by the post-colonial and post-imperial echoes to which we alluded earlier. One critic (M. Griffiths) has argued persuasively that in its portrayal of the country house world of Darlington Hall, *Remains* takes up the myth of the " 'Edenic' garden of the English countryside" in order to adduce the "untidy endings of empire." Whereas nineteenth-century novelists after Jane Austen depicted the country house both as an ideal refuge from urban industrialization and as a "repository of the spoils of empire," Ishiguro's novel depicts the inability of its aristocratic owner to control international politics. Instead of pulling the strings as in former times, Lord Darlington and his kind are the puppets — or, as the professional American diplomat Lewis puts it, "amateurs" (p. 102) — in a world that now controls them. More generally, *Remains* suggests that England and English culture no longer function as the axis around which the rest of the world revolves, a point Ishiguro has emphasized in interviews. Indeed, Ishiguro has pointed to a shared consciousness of England's increasing marginality, in cultural and political affairs, as a major factor in the emergence of a new multiculturalism, or internationalism, in the contemporary English novel. By representing not only the servants but also the masters of the English country house as puppets, Ishiguro simply increases the ironic distance between historical representation and reality to which this novel gives compelling imaginative expression.

Ishiguro's distinctive and original contribution to the multiculturalism of contemporary English fiction comes in the form of a
playful reversal of the myth of "Orientalism." According to the
literary critic and cultural historian Edward Said, with whose *Orientalism* (1978) Ishiguro has revealed familiarity in conversation
with Kenzaburo Oe (1989), European representations of the Orient
have less to do with the East itself than with the Western imagination: "The idea of representation is a theatrical one: the Orient is
the stage on which the whole East is confined. On this stage will
appear figures whose role it is to represent the larger whole from
which they emanate. The Orient then seems to be, not an unlim-
ited extension beyond the familiar European world, but rather a
closed field, a theatrical stage affixed to Europe." Thus the Orient
serves as a dramatic vehicle for conveying and containing European
fantasies of the unknown, the exotic, and the erotic. Despite his
various disclaimers, Said's objection is founded on the view that this
theatrical vision of the East does not match up with reality. What
Said doesn't say here, though he develops the point in his more
recent book *Culture and Imperialism* (1993), is that the theatricality
of representation facilitates a process enacted by texts such as Ishiguro's novels: resistance and reversal through repetition. Ishiguro
hints at such a reversal when commenting to Graham Swift on the
butler's "mythical" status in English culture: "There are certain
things that are very exotic to me about Englishness." By writing in
a style that makes Stevens sound less like an Englishman than like
Etsuko and Ono, the narrators of his "Japanese" novels, Ishiguro
suggests that instead of merely affirming ideologies of cultural nationalism and imperialism, acts of narrative representation may resist or subvert the supposedly natural oppositions on which those
ideologies are built. Instead of giving voice to nationalist consciousness, that is, such acts may be essentially homeless. It is in this
context that Ishiguro's own role as an English novelist is best under-

stood: as an act whose theatricality is both its founding principle and its source of freedom from narrow ideologies. From his impersonation of the role of English novelist, Ishiguro's homeless writing derives its aesthetic motive but also its political force.

REALISM, ANTI-REALISM, AND MYTH

Ishiguro's treatment of these complicated issues of politics and representation provokes further speculations about the problems of realism that we broached in Chapter 1. Ishiguro, we observed, disparages the term "realism" as the mark of a naive and misleading commitment to "journalistic accuracy"—or what George Eliot called a servile creeping "after nature and fact"—that is belied by the ways in which the real world resists such reduction. Instead, Ishiguro emphasizes the value of invention, of refashioning historical reality to reflect the distortions and blind spots that characterize the inevitably limited vision of his utterly ordinary narrators. And yet Ishiguro's fictional worlds are never entirely disengaged from historical reality. It is instructive to note that Ishiguro's objections to Western Orientalism, like Said's, derive in part from its manifest failure to correspond to reality—its inaccuracy, in other words— rather than from a thoroughgoing postmodern skepticism of the very notion of objective representation. It is on such impeccably realist grounds that Ishiguro has aired misgivings about the common European tendency to regard Mishima as the typical representative of Japanese culture. Ultimately, however, Ishiguro's residual but tenacious realism has less to do with notions of solid reality than with their opposite: an apprehension of the perpetually fluctuating nature of reality. It is this sense of flux that Ishiguro captures in the arresting image of the floating world that he employs in the title of his second novel. But instead of sponsoring a postmodern sense of flux, which confronts the reader with competing and logically incompatible levels of reality (as in Rushdie's novels), Ishiguro, like an impressionist painter, installs flux as the quasi-factual ground of his fiction. It is in what Ishiguro calls the "fact" of flux—rather than in the gap that Said perceives between Orientalist representations and material realities—that histories and myths meet to produce what his narrators take to be reality. *Remains* explores the outcome of just such an encounter, and assesses its emotional, psychological, and political impact.

Revisiting Ishiguro's professed anti-realism in this light enables us to understand more fully the role his fiction assigns to myth and myth-making. It is clear in *Remains*, as it is in *An Artist of the Floating World*, that such myths as Stevens's lost England are to be treated warily. Myths may not entirely conquer the flux of reality, Ishiguro suggests, but they contain very real dangers that sometimes leave all too perceptible traces on actual lives. A myth may do no more than temporarily arrest the flux of time and place, freezing it in the memory until one observes how the world to which it seemed to point has drifted out of sight, but *The Remains of the Day* shows how its narrator's life and character are shaped by the myths to which he subscribes—shaped indeed by the process of subscribing to them. In this way Ishiguro reveals how myths—however much they distort the truth, and however much these distortions spoil the lives of their creators (no one, after all, would want to be Stevens)—become inalienable components of our sense of reality. Inevitably, Ishiguro implies, we incorporate myths into our lives and our life-stories, and so make them part of history. The very means by which Ishiguro's invented worlds allow us to dream of freedom from the flux and contingency of historical reality serve also as perpetual reminders of its abiding presence.

The Novel's Reception

The *Remains of the Day* has enjoyed wide success with reviewers and the reading public alike. When it appeared in Britain in May 1989, Ishiguro's third novel was greeted with columns of praise by critics such as Anthony Thwaite and Galen Strawson, and by fellow novelists as different from each other as Salman Rushdie and John Le Carré. "Wholly convincing," John Walsh called it in *The Times*; a "memorable portrait of futility," Thwaite wrote in the *London Review of Books*. According to Francis King in *The Spectator*, *Remains* is a novel of "human warmth" and rare "charm," allied to a "demure wit" and a "rueful pathos." Even *The Economist*, in an article lamenting the "sorry state" of the Booker Prize competition, mustered a note of praise for Ishiguro's *Remains*, describing it as "essentially trivial but exquisitely wrought," and characterizing Stevens as a "memorable and pitiful figure." The Booker Prize itself duly followed, along with sales now totaling more than a million copies in the English language alone. Boosted by the worldwide success of the 1993 Merchant-Ivory film, Ishiguro's most famous novel has also been translated into more than twenty foreign languages.

Remains also won critical and popular acclaim in the United States. It was the first of Ishiguro's novels to do so: the American editions of his first two novels, *A Pale View of Hills* and *An Artist of the Floating World*, had disappeared almost without trace, and in April 1990 Bill Bryson reported in the *New York Times* that the second book had still sold fewer than 2,000 copies. By contrast, the American edition of *Remains* (published by Knopf in October 1989) sold 50,000 copies in its first six months alone. If anything, the novel's reception in America was even more euphoric than in Britain. In the *New York Times*, *Remains* was hailed as a "dazzling novel"; in the *New York Times Book Review*, Lawrence Graver called it a "dream of a book: a beguiling comedy of manners that evolves almost magically into a profound and heart-rending study of personality, class, and culture." *Newsweek* described *Remains* as a "brilliant and quietly devastating" novel, and as a "masterly tragicomedy" bearing comparison with Henry James's tale "The Beast in the Jungle." Favorable notices followed in venues as diverse as *Time*, *The Nation*, *The Atlantic*, *Partisan Review*, and *World Literature Today*.

There was, on both sides of the Atlantic, some dissent. Geoff Dyer, writing in the *New Statesman and Society*, found *Remains* "less impressive" than Ishiguro's previous novels, arguing that while the prose "is as clean and light as ever [. . .] the subtlety has, as it were, become explicit." Dyer contends, moreover, that *Remains* shows that the "whole idea of irony as a *narrative strategy* has[. . .] all but outlived its usefulness," and considers its "poised disingenuousness" to be symptomatic of "much contemporary writing," in which irony "is not ironic enough, never calling itself into question, always immune from its own inquiring, exempt from its own attentions." Gabriele Annan, too, charged Ishiguro with over-explicitness, describing *Remains* in the *New York Review of Books* as a *"roman à thèse"* with a "banal" message: "Be less Japanese, less bent on dignity, less false to yourself and others, less restrained and controlled." In the *New Yorker* Terrence Rafferty echoed the comparisons with James that other reviewers had drawn, but suggested that Ishiguro had learned his master's lesson "perhaps too well and certainly too soon." Like his protagonist, the writer, Rafferty argues, "is shackled by his own expertise, by a helpless obsession with living up to standards"; Ishiguro, he observes, spends all his imaginative energies in "artifice," rather than in an expression of life.

The vast majority of reviewers, however, could find only positive things to say about *Remains*; in a review of *The Unconsoled* in *The New Republic* (1995), Stanley Kauffman ventured the opinion that *Remains* is "perfect." The novel's admirers have tended to focus on three key issues. The first of these was the grace and subtlety of Ishiguro's prose and, as Dyer had predicted, his sure handling of narrative irony. Graver's article in the *New York Times Book Review*, for instance, praised Ishiguro's "command of Stevens' corseted idiom," and remarked admiringly on "the way he controls the progressive revelation of unintended ironic meaning." "The pattern of simultaneous admission and denial, revelation and concealment," Graver added, "emerges as the defining feature of the butler's personality." In *The New Leader* Mark Kamine summed up the critical consensus on this issue with the following statement: "Few writers dare to say so little of what they mean as Ishiguro."

The second major preoccupation of Ishiguro's reviewers was his Japanese background and the way this may have shaped his imaginative vision of England. Several readers — not only the skeptical Annan but also the laudatory David Gurewich, Pico Iyer, Hermione Lee, and Anthony Thwaite — pointed to the indirectness of Ishiguro's style as evidence of Japanese influence. Some readers have approached this issue a little heavy-handedly, asserting, like Iyer in *Partisan Review*, that *Remains* "is a perfectly English novel that could have been written only by a Japanese." While more guarded on such issues, Thwaite, Lee, and Gurewich have all made similar points. Acknowledging Ishiguro's impulse to detach himself from "Western Japanophiles," Thwaite insists that "there are distinct Japanese characteristics (such as indirectness) in Ishiguro's work, however much he may disclaim them." In *The New Republic* Lee dwells on the Japanese elements that unite all three of Ishiguro's early novels, reading *Remains* as an "extraordinary act of mimicry" that only pretends to be an English novel. Citing the similarity between Stevens and the classic Japanese figure of the *ronin*, and pointing to Ishiguro's "un-English insistence on the link between paternal inheritance and honor," Lee argues that it's a Japanese novel "in disguise." Likewise, Gurewich's review in the *New Criterion* compares Stevens's attention to detail with origami, and suggests that the butler's praise of the English landscape's "very *lack* of obvious drama or spectacle" evokes "some of the Japanese criteria for beauty." None of these readers regards the shift from the Japan of *An Artist of the Floating World* to the England of *Remains* as a drastic change of key. Indeed, Gurewich doubts that anyone would have noticed the "fine Japanese sensibility" that imbues Ishiguro's work if *Remains* had been published "under an assumed Anglo name." After reading Ishiguro, Salman Rushdie wonders in *The Observer* whether "England and Japan may not be so very unlike one another, beneath their rather differently inscrutable surfaces."

A third problem frequently alluded to — if not explored in detail — by Ishiguro's reviewers is that of genre. Is *Remains* a comedy, or a tragedy, or a mixture of both — a "tragicomedy," as David Ansen put it in *Newsweek*? In their efforts to answer this question, Ishiguro's detractors have occasionally found themselves agreeing with his admirers. Despite their varying estimates of the novel's worth, Annan, for example, agrees with Gurewich, Graver, and Joseph Coates (*Chicago Tribune*) that despite its formal resemblances to the comedy of manners, *Remains* is really a tragedy. The only significant difference among the critics on this point is that where Annan sees a thesis-novel, readers like Graver and Gurewich discern a subtle exploration of psychological or political repression. Some readers have been more eager to assert the novel's tragic elements: according to Galen Strawson in the *Times Literary Supplement*, *Remains* is a "tragedy of failure of communication" whose pathos is heightened by Stevens's "apparent lack of full humanity." Others have been reluctant to commit themselves: Kamine, for instance, avers that *Remains* is "not quite farce, not quite tragedy." Ishiguro's most insightful reviewers, however, have observed how *Remains* exploits the tension between comedy and tragedy in order to highlight a fundamental problem that faces any reader: how respond to Stevens, and how respond to the tale he unfolds?

During the twelve years since *Remains* was published, the first and second of these topics have continued to preoccupy Ishiguro's readers, who have produced a considerable number of scholarly articles on his work, though only two slight books (of which only Brian Shaffer's *Understanding Kazuo Ishiguro* [1998] is worth reading). Ishiguro's handling of unreliable narration as a means of producing narrative irony is the subject of a lively short chapter in David Lodge's book, *The Art of Fiction* (1992), and of an insightful essay by Deborah Guth in *Forum for Modern Language Studies* (1999). The problem of narrative is also the theme of what is perhaps the single best piece of published criticism on this novel, Kathleen Wall's essay "*The Remains of the Day* and Its Challenges to Theories of Unreliable Narration" (*Journal of Narrative Technique*, 1994). Wall contends that *Remains* "challenges our usual definition of an unreliable narrator as one whose 'norms and values' differ from those of the implied author, and questions the concept of an ironic distance between the mistaken, benighted, biased, or dishonest narrator and the implied author, who, in most models, is seen to communicate with the reader entirely behind the narrator's back."

The question of Ishiguro's Japaneseness, internationalism, and multiculturalism has elicited a wide array of responses. Following up his enlightening interview with Ishiguro in *Contemporary Literature* (1989), Gregory Mason addresses the relationship between Ishiguro's first two novels and Japanese cinema, in a lucid and persuasive fashion, in *East-West Film Journal* (1989). While no serious attempt has yet been made to explore the connections between Ishiguro's work and modern Japanese fiction, various readers have responded to its multicultural implications by interpreting *Remains* as a postcolonial text. Meera Tamaya has some sensible and suggestive things to say on this score in *Modern Language Studies* (1992); Susie O'Brien's ambitious, if sometimes tendentious, essay in *Modern Fiction Studies* (1996) offers some provocative speculations on the politics of Ishiguro's reception, and of the reception of the movie. Perhaps the best article on this subject is M. Griffiths's comparison of *Remains* with V. S. Naipaul's *The Enigma of Arrival* in the journal *SPAN* (1993). Ishiguro's novel, Griffiths concludes, negotiates the "postcolonial condition of England" by employing the "tactics needed to allow the maneuvering subversive right into the house of fiction." Further speculations on such issues may be found in Steven Connor's brief but illuminating discussion of *Remains* in his book on *The English Novel in History, 1950–1995* (1996). Connor's reading of the novel echoes and expands on Rushdie's claim that *Remains* is a "brilliant subversion of the fictional modes from which it appears to descend," by showing how it exploits the possibilities of its own form to make a subtle inquiry into the nature of Englishness.

Of those critics who have examined Ishiguro's treatment of these themes, not all have been entirely sympathetic. A recent essay by

Sheng-mei Ma in *Post Identity* (1999), for example, finds Ishiguro's treatment of his own ethnicity evasive, and interprets the "increasing stylization" of his novels as the sign of a "*reactionary* cooptation into a dream world of postethnicity." The best writing on Ishiguro's handling of such issues, however, is marked by a certain caution that serves as further testimony to the narrative and stylistic subtlety on which so many readers have remarked. Thus, after asking if *Remains* is a "Japanese vision of England or, more slyly, an English vision of Japan," Ihab Hassan observes in *The World and I* (1990) that although for "some readers the suspicion will linger that England and Japan mirror each other at the antipodes," the novel "proves such questions, if not pointless, too stark, for its mode is ambiguous, consummately oblique." But while *Remains* may be, as Hassan suggests, "a subtle allegory of modern history," Hermione Lee implies that even this kind of reading may be insufficiently sensitive to the delicacy of Ishiguro's touch. His novels, like their titles, Lee argues, "hover on the borders of allegory" without ever quite crossing them. Whether they interpret Ishiguro's *Remains* as an attack on colonialism and imperialism, as a diagnosis of the condition of England, as a portrait of sexual repression, or simply as a study of one man's loneliness, Ishiguro's most perceptive readers have responded in some way to what Lee calls the "boundless melancholy that opens out, like the 'deserts of vast eternity' his characters are reluctantly contemplating, under the immaculate surface" of the text.

4

Remains on Film

As most readers are probably well aware, *The Remains of the Day* was made into in a movie that appeared in cinemas all over the world in 1993. Adapted to the screen by Ruth Prawer Jhabvala, produced by Mike Nichols and the Merchant-Ivory team, and featuring a cast that included Anthony Hopkins as Stevens, Emma Thompson as Miss Kenton, James Fox as Lord Darlington, Hugh Grant as Carrington, and Christopher Reeve as the American Lewis, it garnered eight Oscar nominations and numerous other awards, such as the Best Actor awards for Anthony Hopkins from the British Academy of Film and Television Arts, the Los Angeles Critics Association, the National Board of Review, and the London Film Critics Circle (which also named James Ivory Best Director). Box office receipts in the United States alone totaled more than $20 million.

The movie version of *Remains* was one in a series of Merchant-Ivory films that have proved highly popular with cinema audiences everywhere, not least in the United States. Like other Merchant-Ivory adaptations of modern novels, notably E. M. Forster's *A Room with a View* (1986) and *Howards End* (1992), both of which were scripted by Jhabvala (and, in the second case, starred Hopkins and Thompson), the film version of *Remains* seems to have appealed to a certain nostalgia for an idealized England of the past—ironically, the very nostalgia against which Ishiguro's novel cautions us. But if this aspect of the movie indicates insensitivity to one of Ishiguro's most important themes, it is nonetheless worth considering the relationship between the film and the book, if only because the former constitutes the best known and most widely disseminated interpretation of the latter. (Most film-adaptations of novels are, after all, interpretations of the originals, rather than straightforward imitations.)

Many of Merchant-Ivory's changes to the novel lead to simplification, and in some respects this produces an impoverished thematic texture. Some of this simplification has to do, no doubt, with the film-maker's practical imperative to reduce 245 pages of text to a manageable size (at two and a quarter hours, the film is not short as it is); some of it is probably the result of the difficulty of representing in one medium what is portrayed with relative ease in another. A major casualty of the translation from book to film, as Ian Buruma complained in the *New York Review of Books*, is the theme of dignity, which is perhaps more readily conveyed in words than in pictures. In the movie, this theme is briefly introduced by Stevens's father, but its significance in the film as a whole seems minimal. And this revision is not simply the result of the difficulties of translating from one textual medium to another. There was no need, surely, to omit Harry Smith's contribution to the debate on dignity, unless one wanted to flatten out its political dimensions, and thus mute the note of political protest that runs through the novel.

Merchant-Ivory made another, even more important, decision that helped to force dignity out of its central position in Ishiguro's book. Instead of being narrated by Stevens, events are viewed in the movie from a less interested, presumably more impartial, and therefore less deceived point of view—one that corresponds less to first-person fictional narrative than to a third-person account. The film takes certain steps to close down the distance from events that this approach would otherwise create. The opening scene is accompanied by the sound of Emma Thompson's voice reciting her letter to Stevens; later we hear excerpts from Stevens's reply (a substitute for the novel's diary); on a couple of occasions, we find ourselves looking at events through windows and keyholes—ploys that suggest that our point of view is not omniscient but intertwined, to some extent, with Stevens's. So the film scores a limited success in suggesting that the world we see is the world as it is experienced by the central character. But by eschewing the voice-over technique that Martin Scorsese employed so effectively in his 1993 film of Edith Wharton's great novel *The Age of Innocence* (1920), Merchant-Ivory denied themselves the novel's primary means of expressing the theme of dignity: the private musings of Stevens's narrative. In addition to diminishing the political subtext of the novel, the effect of this decision is to over-simplify Stevens's character and also that of Lord Darlington, a complex and melancholy figure in the novel whom the film, as Buruma argues, turns into "a one-dimensional simpleton."

There are other moves toward a damaging simplification in the Merchant-Ivory movie. Lewis, the character played by Christopher Reeve, is a composite of two different Americans in the novel: the senator, Lewis, who attends Lord Darlington's conference, and Farraday, the new owner of Darlington Hall. The effect of this merger is a sharp irony at the expense of Lord Darlington that also makes Lewis look grimly prophetic, as it is he who condemns his English host for amateurism in a new age of professionalism. The price of sharpness, however, is complexity: by keeping Lewis and Farraday separate, Ishiguro subtly indicates a larger sense of historical movement, as English culture finds itself displaced even on home soil by the ascendant American culture of the postwar era. Instead of suggesting this wider tapestry, Merchant-Ivory offer a less nuanced drama of contrasting individual fortunes that also encourages a reactionary nostalgia for a time when England was free of American influence — of its professionalism in politics, its extravagant success in business, and even its cars. In the movie Stevens drives a Daimler and not, as in the novel, a Ford. (This last change is certainly defensible on the grounds that it clarifies the connection between the repressed, repressive Stevens and political Fascism — Daimlers were German-made cars, and Reeves's Lewis tells Stevens that he and the Daimler were made for each other — but its primary side-effect, nonetheless, is to help play down the Anglo-American theme.)

There are several other ways in which the movie makes explicit what the novel, keeping various options open, only insinuates. Here are three examples. First, in a scene that Merchant-Ivory added to the end of Stevens's conversation with Dr Carlisle, Stevens declares that while Lord Darlington made mistakes, he himself is on his way to correct his own (by which he means, of course, his failure to return Miss Kenton's love). This makes it plain that Stevens is quite conscious of something that, in the novel, confuses him to the very end. Second, the movie alters Stevens's last conversation with his father, so that Stevens (who now acquires the first name Jim) hears how his father stopped loving his mother (who is never mentioned in the novel) after finding out that she was carrying on an affair with another man. The point of these changes seems to be to draw a crude parallel between Stevens's relationship with Miss Kenton and his parents' marriage, but the result is a logical non-sequitur. Third, when Merchant-Ivory's Stevens hears Miss Kenton sobbing, he does not, as in the novel, stay outside in the corridor; instead, he enters, and reports yet another error in her housekeeping, a revision that emphasizes the butler's stubbornness and cruelty (just in case we hadn't already noticed them), but that also dismisses the problems of memory that are raised by the corresponding scene in the original version. In the process, the movie sidesteps the challenging questions that Ishiguro's novel asks about literary realism (see Chapter 2).

Yet not all of Merchant-Ivory's revisions of the novel should be marked down as losses. If the complexity of Stevens's narrative is diminished in the movie, Miss Kenton emerges from the shadows to which Ishiguro's narrator consigns her. In Emma Thompson's hands, the housekeeper of Darlington Hall is molded into a convincing and sympathetic portrait of a warm-hearted, generous woman for whom the passing years bring increasing frustration — a frustration for which there is, finally, no remedy. The novel's point, of course, is that Miss Kenton remains in the shadows because the narrator is unable to acknowledge her as a substantial, living person. Ishiguro's Miss Kenton is a figment of Stevens's repressed imagination, a figment that serves a deeper and, for the narrator, more important fantasy of loss. But if Ishiguro's study of the butler's imaginatively impoverished mind is, on those terms, more fully realized than what Merchant-Ivory can show us, a comparison of the two versions does not simply alert us to the primary importance, in the novel, of the narrator's mind; such a comparison also enables us to appreciate that the novel's exploration of Stevens's sense of loss need not rule out an attempt to imagine what Miss Kenton might be like if she were permitted to live.

5

Further Reading and Discussion Questions

This chapter complements the previous four by providing topics for discussion and suggestions for further reading (including relevant websites). Some of these topics grow out of issues discussed earlier, especially in Chapter 2; some questions, especially the last few, introduce problems of a broader and perhaps more challenging kind.

Ishiguro has often stressed the importance of his debt to Chekhov, and has even said that *Remains* was written under the influence of Chekhov's stories. What features of Chekhov's fiction, in addition to the spare, precise style, recur in Ishiguro's novels? Many of Chekhov's stories—"The Lady with the Dog," "Difficult People," and "Enemies," for example—conclude not by resolving a human problem but by clarifying its true nature: do Ishiguro's novels share this tendency?

Although Chekhov and Ishiguro frequently write about similar themes, such as the loneliness and indignity of human existence, do they treat them in the same way? Do particular Chekhov stories call for direct comparison with any of Ishiguro's works on this score? What about Chekhov's "The Lady with the Dog," for example, or the closing sentences of "Neighbours"?

Chekhov's tales are widely available in various editions, including Richard Ford's excellent selection of translations by Constance Garnett, *The Essential Tales of Chekhov* (1998; reissued in paperback, 2000), which also features a wonderful introductory essay by Ford. Readers interested in this line of inquiry might also enjoy Ford's own novels and stories — see, for example, the collection of stories, *Rock Springs* (1987) — as well of those of his great precursor in the fiction of contemporary lower-middle-class life in the American Northwest, Raymond Carver, who is readily available in paperback.

How might one compare *Remains* with other novels in which servants play an important role, such as the Jeeves and Bertie Wooster novels of P. G. Wodehouse, or Henry Green's *Loving* (1945)? How might one compare it with other novels whose narrators are servants, such as Valerie Martin's *Mary Reilly* (1990), which retells the events of Robert Louis Stevenson's *Dr. Jekyll and Mr. Hyde* (1886) from the downstairs point of view? What about Chekhov's "An Anonymous Story" (1893), in which the narrator, whose true identity is never disclosed, poses as a servant? For some interesting critical speculations on this problem in English fiction, see Bruce Robbins, *The Servant's Hand* (1986).

Stevens's pursuit of professional perfection serves as a means of evading other aspects of life, especially the possibility of romance with Miss Kenton, as well as his relationship with his father; in this sense, Stevens's devotion to Lord Darlington displaces the sexual as well as familial aspects of personal life. But are there other ways of considering the relation between the professional and personal aspects of Stevens's existence? Is it plausible, for instance, to consider Stevens's relationship to Lord Darlington not only as a substitute father-son relationship (as I suggested in Chapter 2) but as a surrogate marriage?

What is one to make of Ishiguro's treatment of Fascism in *Remains*, or his treatment of militarism in wartime Japan in his first two novels? How are this political theme and the sub-themes of blindness and betrayal related to the novel's exploration of private life?

Further, what are the implications of Ishiguro's representation of Fascism for his understanding of England? How might one compare Ishiguro's response to this issue with those of other British writers? See, for example, Christopher Isherwood's *Goodbye to Berlin* (1939), which implies that the rise of the Nazi Party is best understood as a response to the various neuroses of Berlin's lonely individuals, who include two prominent English characters: the eponymous narrator and Isherwood's most famous character, Sally Bowles. For a more contemporary and equally brilliant novel that provokes a different kind of comparison on this score, see Martin Amis's *Time's Arrow* (1991), which portrays Nazism as a reversal of the natural order.

An important theme in *Remains*, as we saw in Chapter 2, is the cultural mythology of England. How does Ishiguro's treatment of this theme compare with those of other modern writers, such as E. M. Forster, Evelyn Waugh, or D. H. Lawrence — all writers who, as David Gervais argues in his highly recommended *Literary Englands* (1993), express a deep nostalgia for a lost idealized land? And how does Ishiguro's exploration of nationality compare with those of other contemporary authors, such as Julian Barnes on Englishness in *Channel Crossing* (1996) and *England, England* (1998)? Or with Salman Rushdie's representation of India in *Midnight's Children* (1981)?

A good place to begin further reading on Ishiguro's exploration of this important topic is Steven Connor's *The English Novel in History, 1950–1995* (1996). See also Michael Wood in *The Children of Silence* (1998), which has some eloquent things to say about the problem of stereotyping in Ishiguro's fiction, although Wood is less interested in *Remains* than in *A Pale View of Hills* and *The Unconsoled*.

For a broader, cultural approach to this topic, see Antony Easthope's lucid and engaging *Englishness and National Culture* (1999), which argues that the "most conspicuously characteristic feature" of English national discourse is an empiricism that begins with Bacon, Hobbes, and Locke, and that extends to contemporary writers such as David Lodge. What light does Easthope's argument shed on *Remains*? Should *Remains* be read as a continuation of the English empirical tradition, or does Ishiguro resist it?

Readers interested in pursuing problems of nationality and nationalism through the lens of postcolonial analysis might consult John McLeod's *Beginning Postcolonialism* (2000), which offers an accessible and illuminating introduction to the subject, at the level of both theory and application. There is a vast body of literature on the theory of nationalism, but a useful anthology of some of the most important writings on the subject is John Hutchinson and Anthony D. Smith, eds., *Nationalism* (1994).

How might Ishiguro be compared with contemporary American writers on these grounds? How does Ishiguro's England compare with Raymond Carver's and Richard Ford's treatment of the American Northwest? Or with Cormac McCarthy's representation of the American West in *Blood Meridian* (1985), or Toni Morrison's Ohio in *Beloved* (1987)? Are there similarities in approach or attitude that bind all of these authors together? Or are the differences between them more significant?

Another issue that might be explored more fully, although it hasn't been broached in the critical literature on Ishiguro, is the place of *Remains* in the history of diary fiction. How does Ishiguro's novel relate to other diary novels? Why does Ishiguro turn to this form, and what variations does he play on it? How might one compare Stevens's character with those of other fictional diarists? Does Stevens describe reality, and his relation to it, in the same way as other diarists? How does Ishiguro's handling of time compare with that of other authors of diary fiction? What does Stevens's journal suggest about the nature of writing itself?

Essential reading on diary fiction includes Lorna Martens, *The Diary Novel* (1985), which offers a brilliant historical and theoretical analysis; H. Porter Abbott, *Diary Fiction* (1984), a theoretically-informed discussion that produces numerous sharp insights; and Trevor Field, *Form and Function in the Diary Novel* (1989), which makes a useful contribution to the critical conversation while covering some of the same ground as Martens. In addition to considering some of the questions posed above, all of these critics explore other areas of related interest. Particularly suggestive is Field's claim that the diary novel draws its energy from a crucial tension between fact and fiction — a tension of which the diarist is often aware, and which is heightened in a diary novel because it is a "form of fiction which imitates a factual form imbued with fictional tendencies."

How does Ishiguro exploit the tension between fact and fiction that these critics identify as a central feature of diary fiction? Does he follow a common tendency in twentieth-century diary fiction, which often downplays the realistic properties of the form in order to exploit its potential for invention and experimentation? Or does Ishiguro's fictional practice hark back to earlier models?

Of Ishiguro's numerous precursors in the realm of diary fiction, which authors most invite comparison? What about Tanizaki's *Diary of a Mad Old Man* (1961–62), or Turgenev's *Diary of a Superfluous Man* (1850), in which the narrator is peripheral even to the main events of his life, especially his disappointment in love? Is Stevens a "superfluous man" like Turgenev's Culkaturin?

How are the answers to the previous series of questions affected by Stevens's reliable unreliability as a narrator?

Like Ishiguro's first two novels and his most recent, *Remains* is narrated by an older person looking back over his past. Why is Ishiguro drawn to older narrators? What advantages (and disadvantages) do they seem to have over younger narrators? Should we read these novels as refusals or parodies of the *Bildungsroman* ("novel of development"), which usually describes the early life of its protagonist? In this connection, it might be useful to compare *Remains* with *Bildungsromane* from the late eighteenth and nineteenth centuries — such as Goethe's *Wilhelm Meister's Apprenticeship and Travels* (1796), or Dickens's *David Copperfield* (1849–50) and *Great Expectations* (1861) — and the early twentieth century — Lawrence's *Sons and Lovers* (1913), for example, or Joyce's *A Portrait of the Artist as a Young Man* (1916).

To what large genre (or family of literary forms) does *Remains* belong? Is it, as some readers maintain, a comedy of manners that recalls the high-spirited fictional worlds of Wodehouse, Waugh, and Green? Or is it, as other readers argue, a tragedy of ordinary life (in the manner of some of Chekhov's most powerful stories)? Would we do better to use the term Beckett invented for the subtitle of *Waiting for Godot*: "tragicomedy"? Or is *Remains* best described as a novel in search of a genre?

Most readers detect a clear break in Ishiguro's career between *The Remains of the Day* and its successor, *The Unconsoled*, and regard it as an intentional departure, on Ishiguro's part, from the realism of his earlier work. Do you agree with this view? Are there continuities between *The Unconsoled* and the earlier novels that force us to think again? Is the surrealism of *The Unconsoled* anticipated in *Remains*, or in Ishiguro's other early novels?

Readers interested in this topic might enjoy Andrzej Gasiorek's *Post-War British Fiction: Realism and After* (1995), which doesn't mention Ishiguro, but which does provide a judicious and consistently insightful assessment of the various guises in which the problem of realism has presented itself in recent British writing.

Is *Remains* a postmodern novel, or does it have more in common with the writing of modernist writers such as Ford Madox Ford? For pleasurable as well as comparative purposes, Ford's *The Good Soldier* (1915) is highly recommended. Readers interested in pursuing this issue at a higher level of abstraction will find useful guides to postmodernist fiction and theory in the following texts: Linda Hutcheon, *A Poetics of Postmodernism* (1988) and *The Politics of Postmodernism* (1989); Brian McHale, *Postmodernist Fiction* (1987) and *Constructing Postmodernism* (1992); and, most eloquent of all, Alan Wilde, *Horizons of Assent* (1981).

INTERVIEWS AND WEBSITES

Ishiguro is the subject of several published interviews, of which the following are cited in earlier chapters of this book: with Christopher Tookey in *Books and Bookmen* (March 1986); with David Sexton in *Literary Review* (January 1987); with Graham Swift in *Bomb* (Fall 1989); with Gregory Mason in *Contemporary Literature* (Fall 1989); with Allan Vorda and Kim Herzinger, *Mississippi Review* (1991); with Kenzaburo Oe in *Boundary* (Fall 1991); and with Maya Jaggi in *Wasifiri* (Autumn 1995). The following feature articles have also been consulted: "Profile: Kazuo Ishiguro," *Fiction Magazine* (Spring 1982); Clive Sinclair, "The Land of the Rising Son," *Sunday Times Magazine* (January 11, 1987); Bill Bryson, "Between Two Worlds," *New York Times* (April 29, 1990).

Additional interviews may be located on the internet. Audio and video access to a recent interview with Clive Sinclair is available at *www.roland-collection.com*. Prominent among the topics Ishiguro discusses with Sinclair are creating fictional worlds, growing up in the shadow of the atomic bomb, and the moral crisis of postwar Japan. Another interview (conducted on October 19, 2000) is available in audio at *www.theconnection.org/archive/2000/10/1019b.shtml*. The text of a third recent interview may be found at *www.januarymagazine.com/profiles/ishiguro.html*. An unofficial website for Kazuo Ishiguro at *www.paleview.com* offers further links to news, reviews, and other forms of more or less useful information.

Bibliography

I. Works by Kazuo Ishiguro

Novels:

A Pale View of Hills. London: Faber & Faber, 1982; New York: Putnam's, 1982; New York: Vintage, 1990 (paperback).

An Artist of the Floating World. London: Faber & Faber, 1986; New York: Putnam's, 1986; New York: Vintage, 1989 (paperback).

The Remains of the Day. London: Faber & Faber, 1989; New York: Alfred A. Knopf, 1989; New York: Vintage, 1990 (paperback).

The Unconsoled. London: Faber & Faber, 1995; New York: Alfred A. Knopf, 1995; New York: Vintage, 1996 (paperback).

When We Were Orphans. London: Faber & Faber, 2000; New York: Alfred A. Knopf, 2000.

Stories:

"A Village After Dark." *The New Yorker* (21 May 2001): 86–88, 90–91.

"Family Supper." *Esquire* (March 1990): 207, 208–11.

"Getting Poisoned." *Introduction 7: Stories by New Writers.* London and Boston: Faber & Faber, 1981. 38–51.

"A Strange and Sometimes Sadness." *Introduction 7.* 13–27.

"Summer After the War." *Granta* 7 (1983): 119–37.
"Waiting for J." *Introduction* 7. 28–37.

Miscellaneous:

The Gourmet (film script). *Granta* 43 (1993): 89–127.
Introduction. In Yasunari Kawabata. *Snow Country and Thousand Cranes.*
  Trans. Edward G. Seidensticker. Harmondsworth, U.K.: Penguin, 1986.
  1–3.

II. Select Criticism

Connor, Steven. *The English Novel in History, 1950–1995.* London and
  New York: Routledge, 1996.
Griffiths, M. "Great English Houses/New Homes in England?: Memory
  and Identity in Kazuo Ishiguro's *The Remains of the Day* and V. S.
  Naipaul's *The Enigma of Arrival.*" *SPAN: Journal of the South Pacific
  Association for Commonwealth Literature and Language Studies* 36 (Oc-
  tober 1993): 488–503.
Guth, Deborah. "Submerged Narratives in Kazuo Ishiguro's *The Remains
  of the Day.*" *Forum for Modern Language Studies* 35:2 (1999): 126–37.
Hassan, Ihab. "An Extravagant Reticence." *The World and I* 5:2 (February
  1990): 369–74.
Lee, Hermione. "Quiet Desolation." *The New Republic* (22 January 1990):
  36–39.
Lodge, David. "The Unreliable Narrator." In *The Art of Fiction.* London:
  Penguin, 1992. 154–57.
Mason, Gregory. "Inspiring Images: The Influence of the Japanese Cinema
  on the Writings of Kazuo Ishiguro." *East-West Film Journal* 3:2 (June
  1989): 39–52.
O'Brien, Susie. "Serving a New World Order: Postcolonial Politics in
  Kazuo Ishiguro's *The Remains of the Day.*" *Modern Fiction Studies* 42:
  4 (Winter 1996): 787–806.
Rushdie, Salman. "What the Butler Didn't See." *The Observer* (21 May
  1989): 53. Rpt. in *Imaginary Homelands: Essays and Criticism, 1981–
  1991.* London and New York: Granta Books/Penguin, 1991. 244–46.

Shaffer, Brian W. *Understanding Kazuo Ishiguro*. Columbia, S.C.: U of S. Carolina P, 1998.

Tamaya, Meera. "Ishiguro's *The Remains of the Day*: The Empire Strikes Back." *Modern Language Studies* 22 (1992): 45–56.

Wall, Kathleen. "*The Remains of the Day* and Its Challenges to Theories of Unreliable Narration." *Journal of Narrative Technique* 24:1 (Winter 1994): 18–42.

Wood, Michael. "Kazuo Ishiguro: The Discourse of Others." In *Children of Silence: On Contemporary Fiction*. New York and London: Columbia UP, 1998. 171–81.